Dedicated to Angie Jackson

Foreword

So, if you've purchased this book, implicit in the title is the notion that the odds are stacked against you. This might be true, but it doesn't mean you don't have any control. Unfortunately, the education system has failed you by not teaching you about financial literacy. Simple concepts like what credit is and how compound interest works. What happens if you overpay your tax liability, or, better yet, what tax bracket are you even in? All these things contribute to your personal finance strategy and should be thought about carefully.

Now, I'm sure at this point you are wondering: who is this guy, and why is he in any position to provide perspective on the subject at hand? I made mistakes and still make mistakes related to my finances to this day. In undergrad, I was the guy that signed up for credit cards to buy things I didn't need and eventually maxed those lines of credit out. It wasn't until after undergrad that I learned that the interest was in the high double digits, and it was compounding daily, luckily my line of credit wasn't that large, but it took me almost two years to pay it off. I was also that guy that took out more than I needed in student loans, so I could get a refund check to splurge on things I didn't need. New TV's and bottles of alcohol for pregame parties weren't necessary, but I spent the money anyway and paid the price for it once I got into the professional world. I told you this to feel assured that everyone makes mistakes and finance is a language even you can learn. Chill out if you're not quite where you want to be money-wise; it's a marathon, not a sprint.

Positioned to Fail lays out every component of your financial journey and will give you the building blocks to get better. The content is delivered in a candid, thought-provoking way that will open your eyes to several strategic approaches that can optimize your personal finance journey and strategy. Far too often, we go through life and don't take the time to take a step back and look at every decision we make has financial implications. From the type of life insurance, we select, 401(k) contributions, if we choose to rent versus owning, to whom we decide our life partner will be. Financial literacy matters and should be taken seriously.

Before I let you get to the good stuff, understand that this process is never-ending. At no point will you feel like you have it all together; however, slow motion is better than no motion. There will always be unexpected expenses, and you will likely never feel like you "make enough'. That is okay. If you have a solid foundation, the ebbs and flows of life will not disrupt much. You will feel good about where you are after you turn these pages. I promise you that.

Adarious Payton

Prologue: Ball Is Life

I was ranked in the top 100 in the country in the popular video game NBA 2K at one point in my life. One of the game's main features is the ability to play against other people from anywhere around the globe. For context, the number of people who compete online is in the hundreds of thousands, so being in the top 100 is quite an accomplishment. An accomplishment that I was not proud of.

The reason I was able to achieve this milestone was that I had time. I had so much time because I was unemployed for eleven months. I recently graduated from college with a finance degree, and I just knew I would get a job right away. I had two interviews the Monday after I graduated. Of course, I didn't get either of those jobs. And for eleven months, I was broke, unemployed, depressed, and doubtful of my skills and abilities. NBA 2K was the only thing that got me through. I'd wake up and play three NBA 2K games, eat, go to the gym, apply for jobs, and play three more games of NBA 2K. I'd occasionally take a break to watch Netflix then play more NBA 2K while applying for jobs. That was a daily routine for almost a year. I'd have interviews frequently, but I got a lot of "After careful consideration, we've decided to move forward with other candidates whose skills and experience more closely align to this position." I interviewed six times at a company my uncle is an executive and still didn't get hired. No connection worked. Just writing about this takes me back to a dark place.

I was a Golf Caddie for seven years. I was waiting for my number to be called one day, and one of the older caddies mentioned how he'd graduated from college years ago and, after failing to secure a job in his field, was working as a casino dealer. I just assumed he had a degree in one of the less marketable fields. Then he said he had a degree in............finance. My heart sank to the floor because I thought I might be in the same situation one day.

Eight months later, I got a job as an assistant manager at Wal-Mart, and it was terrible. The hours were long; the customers were unbelievably entitled, rude, and disrespectful. I oversaw the second most demanding area in the store. As far as first jobs go, it was hard, even though I tried to make the best of it. Every day the customers and my fellow associates chipped away at my positive outlook. I had to get out of there. I tried the same company that I interviewed six times before, and seven was my lucky number. I got a job offer as an Alternative Investment Analyst, and after eleven months of unemployment and eight months of working retail, my career in finance finally started. Fast-forward to today, and life has gone well, but nothing quite like I had expected. Everything has worked out for the best. God's plan is often bigger than we could imagine.

I know what you're saying, this isn't that bad, and there are people way worse, and I sound entitled, but this is my story. I told this story because I felt like this was the best way to start my book. I am a living testimony to whoever might be going through something or feels like they're stuck in life that whatever situation you are going through personally, professionally, or financially, it doesn't have to be permanent.

Chapter 0: It's not your fault

Let me ask you some questions. Suppose you have $100 in your savings account, and the interest rate is two percent per year. Taking advantage of compound interest, over 5 years, would you have more than $100 or less than $100? Second question, would your portfolio be more diversified if you invested in an individual stock or an index fund? How'd you do? Did you know the answers? If I had to bet, I would say that the vast majority of you got these questions wrong. Why is that? I would argue that it's because you weren't taught anything about compound interest or stocks. They probably never taught you, and if they did, they just briefly touched on the topics, and the concepts weren't reinforced. You weren't taught any of this, and it is significantly more important than the Pythagorean theorem or the periodic table.

Our educational system has failed us in ways that only a few of us will ever comprehend. Still, the most crucial way is in not teaching everyone extensive financial literacy. Not only were we not taught financial literacy, but corporations and industries have taken advantage of our ignorance to turn a profit. I know a lot of you either accumulated credit card debt when you were young or during college. Opening that first credit card was just supposed to be for gas and that Wal-Mart or Macy's credit card just for the discount, but many of you abused those cards and haven't recovered since. Many of us bought that brand-new car, and with it came the expensive monthly car note plus the cost of insurance, and it turned us upside down. From student loans to college to credit to savings, none of this is taught to us, and that lack of knowledge is used against us every day.

Politicians sell pipe dreams of "canceling all student loan debt" or "increasing the minimum wage," both of which would be great, but that doesn't address your real problem. For example, increasing the minimum wage doesn't mean too much if you're not good with decision making. People tend to buy more when they make more, but no politician is talking about that part. Would you buy life insurance? Or invest? Or save? Likely, none of the above if you haven't been instructed how to do so properly. The minimum wage is a problem, but it's not the main problem. Americans operating on how things should be versus how they are, I think, is the main problem. Not to say the minimum wage should or shouldn't be higher, but it isn't, so now what? We can make the minimum wage whatever we want, but if the mindset of the people receiving the money doesn't change, then it might as well stay the same. One in three lottery winners go broke within three to five years, so the amount of money you have is not the problem; it's what you do with that money. We're fed false promises and bent truths. We vote for companies masquerading as political parties, not solutions to our problems. Understand that your financial situation is not entirely your fault at all, but you're the only one that has to live with it.

The United States has done a terrible job of protecting its citizens from corporations in the name of capitalism. America has failed its citizens because our financial systems' complexity makes financial education and financial literacy necessary to navigate the predatory waters of capitalism. The things we learn in school are largely not useful for everyday life, which has proven a major problem for your average American. America hasn't bred a culture of financial literacy; financial savvy is a scarce resource, particularly in low income and minority communities.

Explain how we live in a country that allows its average citizen to throw away over $1,000 on average per year into a system built on desperation and ignorance. How do we live in a society that spent close to 71 billion dollars in 2017 on a gamble where the odds of winning are about 0.00000000033%? If you don't know by now, I'm talking about the lottery. Imagine having the knowledge and discipline to understand that this is a scam and putting that $1,000 in an investment account. It might not make you a millionaire, but it's almost a guarantee you'll make more money from that over time than you will have from playing the lottery. Our society has been perverted and exploited in America, and it's disgraceful because they prey mostly on low-income individuals. You won't see a payday loan store in an affluent neighborhood. What's a more egregious crime for a government than to manipulate hope? This country has positioned you to fail, where the rich get richer, and the poor get poorer.

You might be reading this book for a way to get your financial life on track. You might be reading this book to add knowledge, and you might be reading this book to dismiss my opinions or ideas, but at the end of the day, I hope that you'll have a different perspective when you finish this book. I know some of you have given up and feel like this will be your life forever, living paycheck to paycheck not being able ever to retire. Don't give up. Your current financial status is temporary. If you want your life to be, it can get better. You can change your life if you adopt a financially savvy lifestyle. Step one is to forgive yourself for the financial mistakes you've made. Learn from them and not do them going forward. We were all positioned to fail in a system where failure is not an option, so we now must succeed.

Chapter 1: Savings

R&B singer T-Pain noted that at his peak, he had forty million dollars in the bank. A few years later, he had to borrow money to buy his children Burger King. By that example, it should be easy to see that money isn't about how much you have but how you spend what you do have. Having more money clearly does not equal financial literacy. Anyone can become a millionaire, but everyone can't stay a millionaire. See the lottery winners mentioned earlier.

Did you know that 6 in 10 Americans have less than $1,000 in their savings account? Crazy right? But what's even crazier is that this doesn't even account for the percentage of Americans who have no savings at all. This means a transmission blow out, a medical bill, or any emergency would send 60% of Americans into debt or pile on to the debt they already have. Not to mention 50% of Americans surveyed could not come up with $400 in a pinch. The funny thing is that your income level does not matter in this situation. The six-figure salary nurse can have the same issue as the McDonalds cashier. Why would a nurse have the same issue as an entry-level worker? Decisions. The nurse drives a brand-new Lexus and lives in downtown Chicago with monthly student loan payments of $400, owns a Louis Vuitton purse and a plethora of other designer clothes, plus a compulsion to travel and dine out. The cashier working full-time, making minimum wage, might net the same amount of money after expenses. Despite the gaps in their salaries, they are essentially in the same boat. Now I know this is a generalization, but this is how I wanted to start the conversation about saving. While it's over-simplified, it is a reality for many people. I also just want to bring to light all that glitters is not gold. The nurse looks like they're living a life most would envy, and they're as broke as the cashier.

This is a large problem, but the good news is that it is a straightforward fix. Before you get out of any hole, you must realize what got you there. I thought I was making more money than I was spending, but my savings account wasn't moving, and I couldn't figure out why. I looked at my credit card statements to see where my money was going. I realized it wasn't the eating out or gas because I knew I was conscious about that spending already. It was the miscellaneous expenses and auto payments on things I wasn't even using. Hulu and other fees that I didn't account for were slowly eating away, and all the money that could've gone into my savings account. Passive payments and other things we may not be actively purchasing have begun to harm many people's finances. Automatic payments can be both a gift and a curse. After you have a real understanding of where all your money is going, you can determine how much you reasonably can afford to spend, and from there and there alone, you can start saving most efficiently.

A second job is a great way to help you save money. Even if you use your second job to save strictly, that would be great. Imagine how much an extra $1,000 a month would help you. What are you really doing when you're not at work, especially when you are kid-free? For two years straight, I worked 70 hours a week doing my first job from 9 am-5 pm, then worked driving for Uber as my second job from 5 pm-10 pm every day, Monday through Sunday. It was non-stop, and my extra income strictly from Uber paid for my rent, utilities, and car note, and I even had some leftover. Imagine that for your life. Now I know some of you have kids or other responsibilities, but for those that don't, save as much of your money while you can. It's plenty out there, so what's an extra 10 hours of work a week? You waste that sitting on the couch, playing video games, or watching reality TV anyway.

You want to save between 10-20% of your income, so for every $1,000 you make, you're putting at least $100-$200 into your savings. I know it's a lot for people with other high expenses, but you must find a way to make cuts somewhere. The point of saving is for the future, and the future is unpredictable. It would help if you had your personal nest egg or at least a rainy-day fund of six months of expenses. That 10-20% you've been putting away accumulates, and then you can practice self-care by being pro-active about potential future financial setbacks. To save money while everything is running smoothly sets you apart from a large portion of a mostly reactive population. You won't wait until something happens to try to come up with the money because you'll be prepared. This is called being proactive. "I am putting away money now when everything is going fine, so when shit hits the fan, because it will, I am prepared" that is why you save for the future. I promise you will save yourself time and stress this way. If you have a hard time doing this on your own, the way your company direct deposits your check can go to different accounts, so 80% of your check goes to your main account, and the rest goes to a side account, so it takes the manual work out of it. This is using the technology that has given us the auto-payment system to your benefit. A good idea would be to look to a money marketing account, a hybrid of checking, and a savings account. This gets you a higher interest rate on your money than a traditional savings account, but you need to start and maintain a minimum balance depending on which company you go through. You also are allowed a minimal number of checks and transfers per month without fees. This can be a good saving and investment vehicle for nest eggs or make big purchases less burdensome.

Saving is nothing without budgeting. A solid monthly budget where you are accounting for your money and having a visual of where your money is specifically going is essential so you can adjust to stay on track. Tons of apps will help you save money. Digit is one I like because it automatically takes the money out of your account based on your spending habits and saves it for you. You do absolutely nothing, and you are saving without thought. Now with any savings account, the key is not to touch it. You can also have multiple savings accounts for different purposes. One for a rainy day, one for saving toward a new car, and one for a house or whatever fits your life. The most important advice I can give you when saving and spending is if you can't afford it twice, don't buy it.

Chapter 2: Investing

When people think of investing, they usually think of the stock market or real estate. But you can invest in anything from gold, weed, cryptocurrency, bonds, even purses, and a ton of other things. What you decide to invest in depends on how much risk you're willing to take on. For example, if you invest in a safe investment bond that won't produce much money but has low risk. Investing in something like cryptocurrency is a high risk but high reward. While these are just about the two ends of the investment spectrum, there is a lot of range in between. If you want something potentially more profitable than a bond but less of a gamble than exchanging your money for cryptocurrency, there are many options available to you. Buying wine and watches can even be great investments, as an investment is nothing more than something you can buy that will become more valuable in the future. My father has an extensive collection of comic books and action figures. This is something he is interested in, which usually helps when investing in uncommon mediums as it takes a lot of knowledge and work. Passion really helps when it comes to unique investments because it's based on your feelings and others like you, unlike money markets. When collecting or investing in uncommon items, you shouldn't do it because you think it will be profitable but because you have a genuine interest in it. This includes your network of family and family and friends as well. Everyone can even invest jointly to run and fund the business if you want. This is how start-ups are formed. Say someone wants to start a business with something their interested in and knowledgeable about but don't have the money to fund it, but you do. Their skills and knowledge with your capital create a mutually beneficial partnership.

A newer version of investing is through Peer-to-Peer lending. Sites like Lending Club and Prosper provide this service. It boils down to loaning people money and getting payments back with interest. Much like how a bank loans to a person, you, along with a pool of people, can loan money to someone who potentially can't or doesn't want to go through a bank for whatever reason. That is essentially the risk as they may not be able to pay back the loan, but you can choose what or whom to invest in. Real estate is a tried-and-true investment option. This is a fascinating and enticing option as there are multiple ways to invest in real estate. Owning your home is not really seen as an investment, but it is as it appreciates and deprecates in value. I am in the process of buying property right now, and I've been thinking about purchasing a multi-family unit where I can live in one unit and rent out the other and be a landlord. If all worked well, this could effectively pay off the mortgage of both units living for free and still building equity because I'm the owner. While this can be a lucrative investment opportunity, there are downsides.

Airbnb has become increasingly popular as well. In the right markets, Airbnb can be very lucrative. You can use your current house, which you live to host guests or buy a separate property to host guests in other locations, you don't live in. This is also a viable option if you are a landlord and can't get a consistent tenant. When you're waiting for a tenant to sign a lease, you can Airbnb the vacant unit. If you'd like to invest in real estate but don't necessarily want to own property, there are real estate ETFs and mutual funds. This is not an exhaustive list of real estate-based investments, and there are quite a few that are more interesting, but if this too is an avenue. Once again, choices, where you may have the expertise, are perfect.

Of course, when investing, never put all your eggs in one basket. Diversification is being invested in multiple areas to decrease your risk. The more diversified you are, the safer you'll be. This ensures that you are protected when downturns happen in whatever market you're invested in, whether it be the real estate market or the stock market. Your age is a good benchmark for how much risk you should take on. The older you are, the more you should invest in safer options. When you are younger, you have more risk tolerance because you have more time to wait out the natural ebbs and flows of market fluctuation. Hiring a financial advisor is something you should start with before investing in everything because they are trained professionals with more knowledge than the average person, especially those beginning their investment journey. A reputable company like Northwestern Mutual or Edward-Jones Financial will have plenty of advisors with a lot of general knowledge. They are salesmen, so you must do independent research as well. Keep one hand on the wheel, because it's still your money and your future, so nobody will care about it more than you.

Chapter 3: Stocks

I'll give you a few things to know so you can pick a good stock. First, you want to look at the company's sales and earnings growth. Second, look at their free cash flows than their competitive advantage. Next, look at their most recent valuation. After that, look at their return on invested capital. Finally, the last and most important thing is to realize that you're not going to do any of those things I just mentioned. Chances are you don't know what those things are, how much time it takes to find them, or even where to look in the first place. In all honesty, I bet some of you stopped reading after I mentioned the first thing. Picking stocks the right way is not, and I repeat, is not for the average person.

Even investors that say buy a certain stock because it's going to explode aren't always right. There are some exceptions to this rule, but generally, it's a crapshoot. For example, Apple and Big Lots offered stock in the same year, some people picked Apple, some people picked Big Lots, and almost forty years later, let's just say one is doing much better than the other. Nobody knows what the future holds or which companies will be here or not in the next 10-20 years. I think we all remember Blockbuster. If you don't, ask your parents. If they don't know, then that means this book has stood the test of time, and then Google what Blockbuster is. Which……... Google might not exist either at this point. The point being companies come and go.

The number one question I get is, when is it going to make money? That one share of that $50 weed stock you bought isn't going to move that much in two weeks or three months, and it can't just be one share either you'd have to keep investing in that company. Then you take it out because it doesn't do anything. Investing is a long game for the most part. If you've ever seen an oak tree, you should know it started as an acorn.

You don't need a lot of money to start investing in individual stocks but be aware of commission fees that your broker might charge and that you can find brokers who don't charge commission fees. If you have to have some stock, make sure you diversify yourself and don't put all your eggs in one basket. Buy stock in companies with products you enjoy, like Starbucks, Nike, or Apple. Where you buy a stock is entirely up to you. For more advanced individuals, you can use something like TD Ameritrade or Scottrade. For beginners, I'd stick with Robinhood. It's purely app-based and is very user friendly. For beginners without a lot of money and who want to get in on the stock market, Acorns is something I like. Acorns is what you call a Robo-advisor. What it does is you connect your bank and debit or credit cards, and for every purchase you make, it takes the change and rounds up to a full dollar. So, if you spend $5.40, Acorns will invest the remaining $0.60 into an investment account. This account is a portfolio of ETF's or Exchange-traded funds, which is just an investment vehicle that invests in certain types of companies. One ETF might contain a little Apple and a little Microsoft and a basket of other similar stocks. They are essentially exposing you to a wide range of stocks. As you get more advanced and more involved in the investing world, you can upgrade to other ETF's like SPDR or GLD, or EEM. Overall, ETF's are the way to go, in my opinion, as opposed to stocks, but please do your research before investing in anything. Never try to time the market. If you see that the DOW has been declining over the past week, don't wait to invest. Timing the market is hard, one and even harder to be right about, so just get in when you're ready. Regardless of what you invest in, it's all related to the Dow Jones and S&P500, so it's good practice to know what the stock market is doing. The Dow Jones measures the performances of the thirty largest publicly traded companies in the United States, and the S&P 500 measures the 500 largest publicly traded companies in the United States. These are like indicators of how the overall market is performing. However, just because the Dow Jones or S&P 500 is up or down doesn't necessarily mean your stock is up or down. I get a notification from an app every morning telling me if the DOW opened higher or lower than the previous day. And by how much and why it changed. The stock market and investing in stocks and ETF's can be daunting, but only because you're not familiar with it. With a few baby steps and a little research, you can get the ball rolling toward good returns.

Before you get invested in the stock market with individual stocks, you should do a few more things first. First, invest 15% into your 401(k) and/or IRA for retirement. Next, invest in some funds focused on growth, growth and income, aggressive growth, and international funds. Growth Funds are mid-cap funds with mid-sized companies. Growth and Income Funds are large-Cap funds, which contain bigger companies like Apple, Wal-Mart, and Microsoft. Aggressive growth, which are small-cap funds with smaller companies anticipated to grow bigger and international funds are companies outside of the United States. Best practices suggest putting 25% of your money in each and keep contributing to them periodically. After you've covered those bases, then start picking individual stocks. This order is best because you cover long-term investing for your retirement with your IRA & 401(k), then some safer investing with those four funds I mentioned. Finally, some money to take a little risk with individual stocks.

Chapter 4: Millionaire Status

If you had to guess what are the top professions with millionaires, what would you say? Doctors or lawyers or investment bankers or actors? Something like that? What if I told you that teachers are in the top three professions with the highest percentage of millionaires? With one and two being engineers and accountants respectively. Well, it's true. Twelve to fourteen percent of teachers are millionaires. That is one of the occupations with the greatest number of millionaires. So, for every 100 teachers, twelve to fourteen of them are millionaires. I'm not lying; look it up if you don't believe me. It's surprising when you think about it because teachers are known for their humble salaries, but certain circumstances help them become millionaires. The point of me saying that is because there are a lot of myths and misconceptions around millionaires. Most believe that they are only in certain glamorous professions and either went to elite schools, got high-paying jobs, inherited their money, or all of them. While that does happen, it's only a small percentage of individuals that become millionaires this way. Most millionaires are just like you. Millionaires come from humble beginnings. They might never crack a six-figure salary or inherit any money. I'm sure you have a neighbor or two that are millionaires, and you'd never guess. The perception of millionaires is based on how they are portrayed in the media, far from millionaires' reality. Most millionaires don't even have multiple luxury cars parked in front of a three-car garage home. Again, that does happen, but for most, that isn't the case. The only thing that millionaires almost consistently do is be college graduates, but that is not a barrier. You could do it too, even if you didn't earn a 4-year degree. A useful education, discipline, and good decision-making skills are all you need.

If you don't leave behind at least a million dollars, you've done your family a severe disservice. In all honestly, solid decision-making and a little good fortune are all it takes to leave meaningful wealth to your kids. I want you to forget right now that you don't make a six-figure salary, didn't inherit any money, and didn't go to an Ivy-league school. A meager salary is no excuse for why you can't become a millionaire. Living below your means is a good start. If you are operating your life on your full take-home pay, you live paycheck to paycheck. Living off $3/4^{th}$ of your salary where the other $1/4^{th}$ goes to a nest egg is the simplest way to get on track.

Credit cards, car loans, and college are all debt, and we've all been conditioned to accept debt, but we don't have to be. With debt, there is interest. If you think about it, you're paying someone to borrow money for something you can't afford. What if you just saved money to buy things instead?

Now, if you're an average Joe, that might mean conditioning yourself to seek out more affordable options. Like buying a used car with money you saved up instead of getting a car loan, so it's all cash and no debt. This means no interest and no chance of repossession or being upside down. Now obviously, that car probably won't be as new, and that's kind of the point, but you're getting exactly what you're paying for as opposed to paying for more than you're getting. You avoid both paying interest and risking a lower credit score. Going to junior college to start and getting your general education courses out of the way, then transferring to a 4-year college or university to finish often saves people tons of money. Even if you have to take out student loans to finish, the amount will be significantly reduced compared to starting at a 4-year college or university. You also may not have to live in on-campus housing because you'll come in as at least halfway done, which is a money-saver as well. This frame of thinking will keep you out of debt and out of interest payments. For my college loan, I've paid back more in interest than I have in principle. Most importantly, there's no risk of defaulting on loans and credit cards because you won't have any. Debt is the biggest hindrance to becoming a millionaire, and this is how you can avoid it by making better decisions.

Deciding to have children is a significant financial commitment, and the more you have, the more money they cost. My mother owns a home daycare, and her prices are on the lower end. One day we looked at a child she's kept for three years and how much the child's mother has paid to just my mother alone, and it was over $20,000. That's not including clothes, food, and activities. Imagine having $20,000 saved or invested. What if you had two children? Then you'd double that. Children are the most expensive decision you can make, and they can and will hinder your financial situation if you are not prepared for them. It's important to know and understand children are a choice whether it's the decision to take the condom off or keep it on. Obviously, the best case is abstinence but let's be honest here. Earlier I said the rich get richer and the poor get poorer but, it's really the rich get richer, and the poor keep having babies. Children are a blessing but only when you're ready for them. Other than that, they are a burden. I truly believe that we irresponsibly assume our children will be healthy, which is not always the case. Those children might have special needs, which can cost more money than a healthy child. The department of Agriculture estimates by the time your little ~~accident~~ bundle of joy turns eighteen, you'll have spent around $233,610 raising them. Like I said about that $20,000 for childcare over three years, a mother and/or a father found a way to come up with that money. I bet if they didn't have that child, they still wouldn't have managed to save that $20,000, but they found it for what was necessary. Make saving necessary.

When people make more money, they spend more money and don't account for severe shifts in their lifestyle. This is the main reason the high salary professions we think should obviously produce millionaires at as a high rate as we'd expect do not. It is purely based on decision-making and some luck. A lot of poor decisions I see stem from overspending on things we really don't need. Especially in the age of social media, many things are purchased for the express intent of impressing other people. It's the concept of keeping up with the Jones' on crack. This is not to bash millennial culture because status signifying has been around for a long time. Due to modern social influences, the Millennial and Gen Z portions of the population have a severe case of FOMO or Fear of Missing Out. While society has always dictated where people think they should be in their current stage of life. Social media has taken that idea and increased it 100-fold. Before social media, society was mostly limited to your surroundings, comprised mostly of people at work, church and school, and your neighbors. Now society is the whole world because of how connected we are through social media. The thing is in every generation with social media or not, nobody knows how anyone got anything, nor do they know how much they paid for it or what they had to do to get it or what they're doing to keep it, and people are comparing their lives to what they see. In terms of social media, everyone is "The Jones'," and everyone is poor at the same time. All you see is a highlight reel, but very few people are posting their mistakes. What you see is the newest BMW. You don't see the $750 car payment over six years with the $250 monthly insurance.

I was in a neighborhood with some of the biggest houses I've ever seen. These were mansion-sized homes with multiple luxury cars outside. While I was in awe, I also asked myself, who needs that much house? Now I'm not at that level financially, so maybe I can't understand why someone would need that much house, but to me, it looked like a huge waste of money. Again, I'm not in their shoes, but I know for sure there are rooms in those houses that probably aren't even inhabited. This is a large example, and if you scale it down to your situation, you can apply it to something like how many clothes you own or how often you eat out. Do you really need that many clothes? Would it drastically alter your lifestyle to spend less money on clothes, or would it kill you to pack lunch now and then? Simply because you can, doesn't mean you should. My version of this is traveling. You can argue traveling is an experience, and your money will return, which is true, but financial goals should trump how cavalier you are with your money every time.

Financial goals are the best way to stay on track and to help plan for your future. I think the best way to start your financial goals is to start backward, plan for retirement first, and work your way to the present. What do you want your life to look like in your senior years? When do you want to retire? Do you want to retire early? Do you only want to work part-time as you get older? These are more long-term goals, but they help you shape your short-term goals. For short-term goals, which are no more than two years in advance, what do you want those to look like? My goal one year was to have $20,000 in the bank by the end of the year. Another goal was to pay down half of my student loan debt in two years. It's not the worst thing if you don't hit your goal. A hospital visit can alter goals quickly, but you know what you were aiming to do, and if life does happen, at least you were tracking towards something. Having a target to aim at will keep you on track no matter what life throws your way.

Investing is a great way to give your savings a substantial boost. 401(k) and Roth IRA's are great resources, which I will get into later, but these are two common tools that millionaires use to achieve their million-dollar status. Contributing to your 401(k) and receiving the company match is just common sense in most cases. Depending on your career, you might have access to other retirement vehicles. I know teachers can take advantage of a 403(b). When saving for retirement, 15% is the magic number. 15% of your income should be going to your retirement, which could be 6% in a 401(k) to get the match, max out a Roth IRA, then whatever else will get you to 15%.

Much like I said, it's all decision making one decision you must make is working harder. A second job or passive income will do wonders for your short- and long-term financial goals. If you are intentional with a second income, financial problems become less and less existent, but you must work. Laziness is not a characteristic of self-made millionaires. Trust me, a 9-5 five days a week is not easy, especially depending on what you do, but you have to see it as investing in yourself. This is the work you must put in to reach millionaire status. Before I started doing Uber, I'd go to work, do my 9-5, then go home and cook dinner, sit on the couch, play a few video games and go to bed, and on the weekend float around the house then maybe go out for a drink later that evening. Looking back, a great waste of time. Now I don't intend to work this hard forever because it's not sustainable, and I also won't have to because of what I put in place to where every decade, I make more money and work less. If your current space in life doesn't allow you to have a second job, you can better manage your expenses. Maybe you don't need cable and can get by with Netflix. Maybe you don't need Netflix, Hulu, and Disney+ or a TV to begin with. Either way, something has to give whether you get another job, or you cut your expenses. It took time to get this millionaire mindset, but I never let go once I got it. If you don't want to be a millionaire, that's fine but ask yourself, why not? I just detailed why it's not hard, and all you have to do is a few simple things.

Chapter 5: Life Insurance

I bet you think that you're set since you have life insurance through your job. WRONG DO NOT PASS GO DO NOT

COLLECT $200. Your life insurance policy through your job will only be one or two times your salary on average, which is nothing over time. This is group life insurance. It's essential to have at least ten times your salary. If you make $50,000 a year, you need $500,000 in life insurance, especially if you have a significant other and/or children. Not only that, if you become no longer employed, you no longer have life insurance either. In the case of your unfortunate death, a GoFundMe can't be your life insurance policy supplement, and if it is, I'm not donating to it because I told you what to do, and you still didn't do it. Funerals are expensive, and people tend to become grandiose when mourning. We've all experienced someone's death and gone to their funeral, and you see a billion flowers that aren't cheap, and the casket was more expensive than your car, then food for the repast and a headstone. You name it, it costs money, and this is all before you're in the ground. We've all had loved ones leave this earth, and it's hard to deal with emotionally. Now add in the financial struggle that you might've been in before they passed. Now you must come up with the money you don't have to bury them. You'll be worse off than where you were before. Let's not forget that you also have to figure out how you will replace that income potentially. Now let's inject an individual life insurance policy in this scenario. And we can even be modest. Let's say your deceased husband, wife, son, daughter, mother, or father passes away, but they have a $150,000 life insurance policy. The funeral costs are covered with some money left over after it's all said and done. Even if the funeral costs $30,000, you have $120,000 leftover. The extra money you leave behind could pay off a house, lingering student loan debt, college fees for someone, or just the cost of living.

Your death should not become a financial burden for your loved ones. If you leave this earth and do not leave your survivors, anything you have done the people you love a severe disservice and can have ramifications for years to come. If you have that life insurance policy, the final gift you give your loved ones is the best thing you could give. Bottom line, you're going to die, and you don't know when so prepare and prepare correctly now while you're alive and well.

I think it's best to get life insurance as soon as you can because the younger you are, the less likely you will have health problems, which equals a lower premium, but as time goes on, you're more likely to develop sickness' or conditions. As a result, insurance companies will charge more to insure you, if at all. Not only sickness but also poor lifestyle habits will impact your ability to get insurance. They go through your history in quite a bit of detail, from credit score to driving history, because these are indicators of how much of a risk you are. Not to mention that poor eating habits or smoking increase your likelihood of diabetes, high blood pressure, hypertension, lung disease, etc. Insurance companies charge you higher amounts due to this or won't insure you, as your lifestyle indicates what they deem to be an unfavorable risk. They know this because they will send a nurse to give you a checkup to get a good amount of life insurance. She will draw your blood, take your blood pressure, and weigh you to calculate your body mass index to verify if they can be insured or not. I'm sure that your job insurance policy did not get all this information because the amount you're receiving from them isn't that much. It is also essential to get a guaranteed insurability rider. This addition will allow you to buy more insurance without proving your insurability. When you die, you'd like your survivors to have the maximum amount of money possible, and this is great if you develop a condition that would normally deem you uninsurable. The amount you can add is relative to the policy amount you already have, so you can't double or triple your policy amount.

I'm 28 years old, and I got a ten-year term life insurance policy at 25. Fortunately, I did not have any health problems and a healthy lifestyle at this time, so I am considered preferred elite, so I am fully insured for $500,000 at a $50 monthly premium (that's just one night out to dinner) for 10 years. Obviously, I want to outlive this policy, and chances are I will, but in ten years, I'm going to need another policy, and this where it gets tricky. The three options available to you after your term life policy expires depend on your individual circumstances. The best possible scenario is that at the end of your ten-year period, you simply start a new policy where you take another exam to prove you are still in good health. This premium will be higher because you are older, but the increase will be nominal if you are in good health. The second option is to convert your term policy to a permanent policy, which will still be covered, but your premium will be more expensive. The last option is to extend the policy to a year-to-year basis where the coverage you have is the same, but the premium you pay monthly substantially increases. This is beneficial for you if you can't qualify for another policy due to your inability to prove good health. This is also for you if you have a terminal disease and you'll only be paying that high premium for a few years, then it's worth it. For example, say your policy is up today, and you've been given less than three years to live that high premium might be worth it relative to the death benefit your family receives at your passing.

There are several types of life insurance; some similar and some completely different. I can't tell you which one to get, but a life insurance professional can help you out. Term life insurance is what you would call a pure insurance policy because your beneficiaries are only receiving a benefit at your death. Generally, these policies range in coverage from 10-30 years and are very cheap. Usually, 5% of the policy is what you pay in premium through the policy's life. Whole life insurance is an insurance policy where your beneficiaries receive money at your death. It has a cash value, which means some of the money you pay monthly in a premium goes into a pool where you can borrow money from tax-free. Still, you're essentially borrowing your own money and potentially paying interest on it depending on how the policy was written or the type of policy. Not only that, but you're also paying up to 10 times as much money compared to a term life policy for the same amount of money at your death. So, a $500,000 term life insurance premium might cost $50 monthly, but a whole life policy for the same amount can cost $500 monthly for the same amount of death benefit of $500,000. Whole life does last forever, even if you stop paying on the policy and you will be in a paid-up status where you still have the death benefit and the cash value up to the amount when you stopped paying, which is different from the term life, which lasts a set amount of time. Universal life is the same as whole life but is a little more flexible because you can change the premium and death benefit without getting a new policy. A variable life insurance policy is like a whole life policy. It has investment benefits like a mutual fund where your beneficiaries get a cash benefit at your death and decent gains like you would for a mutual fund. For older folks, guaranteed issue whole life insurance is insurance that you don't necessarily have to prove good health, but with that, premiums can get expensive. This is mainly for an older person with declining health. These are the policies you see commercials for during the price is right or afternoon soap operas when older people tend to be at home. Final expense insurance is exactly what it sounds like. It's for your final expenses, so funeral cremations and last medical bills, etc. This is really for older individuals who don't have any other insurance or money saved up but don't want to burden the family with their final expenses. Finally, group life insurance is what you have through your job, which covers your salary between one to two times. Again, this is generally not enough coverage. It is not free or cheap, so it doesn't hurt to get it but know it's not enough money. And like I said, if you lose that job, that policy is no more, so you'd want this and a personal policy as well. For children, don't buy them life insurance; there are better ways to save money for your children without the costs associated with life insurance. What you can do is buy them a rider to your insurance plan. Many companies will advertise that this is a great way to save money for the future because it grows tax-deferred, but there are many costs associated with life insurance plans, so a better use of that money would be to invest.

Chapter 6: Long term disability

This might be the most important chapter in the book. The odds of you suffering a disability before retirement are one in three. That's high. Between you and your two best friends, one of you is likely to become disabled. Statistically, none of you will have adequate insurance to weather this hit to your income. This is the most important chapter because the most important thing in your life is not insured. You are the most important thing in your life and your ability to work or your working capital. Do you have car insurance, homeowner's insurance, cell phone insurance, but not disability insurance? Say you're in a bad car accident and can no longer work or produce income. What will you do? You will most likely struggle. Maybe you'll get a little money here and there from loved ones, but that's no way to live. You already don't have an emergency fund, but how long will that sustain you while producing no income even if you did? An emergency fund isn't designed to do that, but long-term disability insurance is. The idea that it couldn't happen to you is an ignorant way of thinking. We must get out of our own heads as much as possible. Just think about how much of a blow to you and your family a loss of income.

Many of you have a short-term disability through your jobs, and that is good, but that will only cover one to three months of around 80%-100% of your income. Long-term disability will cover years of around 50%-60% of your income. It is important to have both due to what's called an elimination period. An elimination period is a time between when the claim is made and the time before you can collect on the long-term disability insurance. Short-term disability will take care of you in that period. It's a few things you want to consider when buying a policy. The very first thing would be to check to see if the company you work for already offers long term disability and how much of your income they'll cover because most likely it isn't enough. But it's good to know how much anyway since you're paying for it. Even if you do have long-term disability insurance through your current job, it might not be the case at another job. If you change companies or lose your job, it might still be a good idea to have a separate policy. Three words to look for in your policy are non-cancellable, own occupation, and partial benefits. Non-cancellable just means the terms you agreed to don't change. Own occupation means that you still get paid if you can still work but not at the same occupation. So, say you're a surgeon like Doctor Strange and suffer a terrible hand accident and can no longer be a surgeon. Instead of becoming the master of the mystic arts, you become a college professor, and you will still get paid from your policy. Residual benefits are similar, but this means that if you can't work full time anymore but can work maybe part-time, then you'll still get paid out from your policy. Your benefit period should be up to retirement age, which will make the policy more expensive, but it's worth it. I talked about the elimination period before, but this can be long or short. The shorter it is, the more the premium, and the longer it is, the cheaper the premium. Your short-term disability should take care of you during an elimination period, so if you have that, then you can stretch your elimination period out to the length of your short-term disability. After that, you should be set and pray you never have to use it.

An old co-worker of mine was in a car accident and developed fibromyalgia and is in constant pain. She said her work disability insurance is limited, but her personal policy makes up the rest of her income. That is a mild example because she can still work, but it could've been worse. Please don't think it can't happen to you because what if she thought that and didn't get a personal long-term disability policy? She'd be in a tough spot with two kids, but she is covered because she had foresight.

Chapter 7: Student Loans

$1.8 trillion. 44 million. $37,000. The first number is how much student loan debt we've accrued nationally. The second number is how many Americans have student loan debt. The final number is the average amount of student loan debt. These are daunting numbers, and let's be honest, most of us got scammed. I always think about what if the government gave me the money for my four-year college's total cost and put that in a mutual fund. For the time it would take for me to pay that amount back, how much money would that be? College was overprescribed, and trade school or going straight to work after high school was socially shunned upon. Even the way certain trades are perceived in the media force us in a certain direction. For example, when you see a plumber in media, they're often overweight, sloppy, butt crack showing while a doctor is clean-shaven, fit, and polished. If that's not social engineering, I don't know what is. Having a college degree was portrayed as the golden ticket to a life of financial stability and success but was it the best idea? Imagine how much money and less debt you'd have if you would've started working right after high school instead of four or more years of higher education or went to trade school for a year or two and picked up an actual skill instead of going to college. Doing this instead of taking out debt for school, would you be better off? The answer for some of you the answer is no, but for many of you, the answer is yes. I have a bachelor's in finance, so my earning potential is relatively high, but that's not the case for everyone with a finance degree or in general. Generally, a college degree does not guarantee anything but student loan interest and debt. It probably wasn't worth $100,000 in student loans to learn things you didn't need but good memories. I bring this up not for you but so the generation after you is not perverted by the idea of college. Trade school and junior college should not be viewed as bad options at all. Social pressure with the government's help tricked us all, but we must first fix it within our own community before the problem can be fully remedied. Now I'm not against college. I lied, I am for reasons I won't get into, but we should start shifting the conversation to lucrative majors in tech and nursing and not these degrees with low earning potential. It's not that the degree makes little money; it's the fact that it costs a lot of money to attain the degree that pays little money. My sociology professor with his Ph.D. was also a part-time grocer, and he loved what he did; and I really enjoyed his class, but the pay did not justify his career path. College isn't for everyone, and it's too expensive to see if it is or not. 40% of people who go to four-year institutions do not graduate within six years, so now they're with no degree because college wasn't for them or wasn't for them at the time. But college was forced down their throat, so they had to go and struggle and are still in debt. We must get out of this mindset and not reproduce this cycle of student loan debt. Women and minorities study low earning subjects, and you get a bachelor's in social work then a master's in social work, and you're $200,000 in student loan debt. Then every job you want says you need years of experience that nobody would have at your age for a meager $43,000 starting salary. Our social addiction to the idea of education has created blissful ignorance because of the severe difference between what a college education is and what it should be.

I would rather have you hate your job and make a good amount of money instead of hating your job and making no money. Again, it's not your fault, especially if you've never had influential people in your life with lucrative career paths or no guidance to show you what this career path will likely be. By the time you find out, you're in too deep, whether in money or time or both. Then the people pushing you to go to college think it's the same cost as when they went to college. We need to be honest about this first to change it or what's stopping us from repeating it. Every four years, there is a candidate promising student debt forgiveness. It's not happening; trust me. Then, even if it does happen, what is stopping this from happening to another generation?

Now that we've gotten that out of the way, how do you get out of debt? The first thing to know where you are currently is how much you have in principle and how much you have in interest. How much have you paid in both as well? It's great to consolidate your loans unless they're federal loans. Income-driven repayment is a great option but do not get caught in that trap for long. Your loan provider wants to keep you a customer for as long as they can to keep getting interest. The next thing you want to do is pay more than they prescribe you, so if they have you paying $175 a month, pay that and add another $25 on top of that. It'll make a world of difference, but you must tell the loan provider that the extra money will be going directly to the principal. If you work in public services, such as a government worker or state employee, you can get your student loans forgiven after 8-10 years of service but don't depend on that as that can change depending on how the government feels that day. The final and most important thing you need to do is look at your expenses monthly and see what you can cut out and put toward your student loans. While I am student loan debt free, I moved out of my parents' house sooner than I should have and got my own place paying $900 a month for two years, which with groceries and bills is roughly around $26,000. I couldn't fathom paying $900 a month to get out of debt, but I easily came up with it for an apartment—the same thing for my car. I leased a brand-new car and was paying $306 a month plus $120 in insurance for the same period. That's another $10,000. I could've been out of debt sooner with a lot less interest paid and have a nicer nest egg if I would've managed my decisions better. Now it's your turn. Look in the mirror and see what you've been doing with your money that could've gone to student loans instead of whatever else you found the money, whether it's a new car or an apt or a lot of traveling or eating out. You could've cut or limited what you did and put that toward student loans, but it was hard, and it is hard to give that money to them, especially if it's your first taste of independence. Look at yourself and make changes to yourself. You know at the core what you should do, but I get it. It's hard.

Chapter 8: Marriage

Let me start by saying I am not married at the time of me writing this, but I did consult several married individuals for this section.

Love is great, but marriage is a business and should be treated as such. Money is the number one thing couples get divorced over, so treating your marriage like a business might be a better way of keeping the love and happiness in your marriage. Understanding that concept shouldn't be something done after you've said I do. That should be done in dating. You should understand how your partner treats money and if that will be a lifestyle, you are comfortable with. Just because they are bad with money while you're dating them should not be the end all be all, but then it's up to you and that other person to be willing to make changes. If that person is resistant to changes or does not want to change for you, then that's a clear sign that they're not the person for you. To be clear, I am not saying one person is better with money or worse; I am asking, does this person generally align with how you look at money? I enjoy my money. I save a good amount, and I always look for a deal because I like my money, but I also enjoy traveling, clothes, and eating well. It'd be crazy for me to date then marry someone who is a loose spender who impulse buys and doesn't save well. On the other hand, someone else could consider my spending too cavalier, so it's all about your point of view.

I think the adage; opposites attract, is very true, especially in dealing with personal finances. Spenders date savers, and savers date spenders. I don't know why that is, and it doesn't logically make sense, but it works that way for some reason. I rarely see a couple that looks at money the same way, but if anything, two bad spenders are together more often than not, it seems like. Generally, no one is particularly good with personal finance, so it's like one is bad, and the other is worse.

I'm a big believer in joint bank accounts in marriage. I look at marriage as a unit and separate bank accounts never made sense to me. I think each should be aware of the money in it and going out of it and planning the decisions you might want to make, like building up a nest egg or saving for a kid's college. It just makes things easier, and it will force you to have conversations with each other more proactively, which will help mitigate impulse buying.

When dealing with finances in marriage, one person should be responsible for the money. I don't think this should be a two-person job. One person should be responsible for managing the cash flow, what goes out through bills and other fixed spending, not necessarily the nickels and dimes for food out or anything but just monitoring the budget, sticking to financial goals adjusting when the unexpected occurs. This should not be a two-person job. It should go to the person who is not necessarily better with money but detail-oriented, mindful, and strategic, usually the person who is better with money. Now, just because one person oversees the money doesn't mean that the other partner doesn't have a say-so or can't input things they think are good ideas because that is still your spouse they have feelings and assuming they work, it's their money is also going into this account so talk through things. Even if they don't work and stay at home, that is still their money. You're married. A marriage is about communication, so talk about the finances too. Those conversations can be hard and take a little practice on both sides, and it should be practiced.

The first and most important thing is understanding how money was looked at and treated in their childhood by their parents. This will be a very telling story of how they came to view money now. Do not identify as "I" and identify as "we/us/our." Instead of I have to get out of my debt. It becomes we have to get out of debt. Discussing goals is probably the easiest way to ease into them. Whether it is paying off the house or getting out of debt or saving for the kid's college, either way, discuss, and then you can put them into action. This is probably just general life advice, but I feel as if we generally don't address what bothers us when it's small and only gets bigger. The conversation about the issue is harder to have because the real problem is layered within previously held in frustrations.

Subsequently, the conversation isn't productive. Avoiding big conversations and having smaller, more intentional conversations will keep things calm and cool. Like everything, there is a time and a place for it. Finances are no different. Having these conversations after a workday is probably not a good idea. Nor is having these conversations a good idea after a big change like a death in the family or moving as its more emotions involved. Pick an ideal time like a Sunday after church. If you're initiating the conversation, don't lead with spreadsheet graphs and thirty-year projections. That is one sure-fire way to lose someone, and it's partially manipulative when you know they're not familiar with any of that. Start with the level you think they are at and grow from there. Tact and willingness to learn are the keys to successful financial conversations. Some people do not like to talk about finances and are unwilling to learn or participate, and that is usually a huge red flag, but you have to find a way.

A common misconception in marriage is that your credit scores are combined. That's not true. Marriage does not combine your credit scores, so you will still have your own credit score unless you open a loan together or a joint credit card. If your spouse does have bad credit or just wants to get better credit, putting bills in their name and paying the bill will help their score increase that way as well, but I think most importantly, sitting with a credit coach will be cathartic for both of you regardless of credit scores. It's always a good idea to consult the experts.

I think that couples should go to counseling before marriage. Spiritual counseling & marriage counseling, but what about financial counseling as well? You're taking a big step together, and let's be honest, it's not cheap to get married and to stay married. Why not be proactive?

You also shouldn't live off both of your incomes. I think your lifestyle should be supported by one or one and a half of an income. I think the person who makes less should be the base for your lifestyle as a couple. Say one of you loses your job gets sick or injured, your lifestyle changes, and since your lifestyle was supported by two incomes, everything shifts. If you're married, pause and ask yourself what would happen if one of you lost your jobs. Not only does living off one income save you from catastrophe, but it's also a great way to save money. Let's say you make $3,000 a month and your spouse makes $4,000 a month, and you live off one to one and a half times your joint income of $4,500 to $5,000, you have $2,500 to $3,000 of saved money a month. Two years into marriage, you've been doing this strategy, and someone losing their job is still tragic, but you have $60,000 to $72,000 saved. There's no reason to panic because there's no significant shift in lifestyle, and you can comfortably look for another job. This is also a good idea for attacking debt where the other income goes to paying off credit cards, student loans, or medical bills.

Over time I've been more in favor of the word partner as opposed to husband or wife. Yes, it's simply semantics, but changing our language is important, and I think this is the best use case of that. Marriage is a business, and you wouldn't go into a business with someone you don't think could keep the business afloat. Why marry someone that you know you wouldn't go into a business partnership with? Marriage is simply finding the right partner to make you better, grow your wealth, and raise a family. It's important to find the right partner but, more importantly, to be the right partner.

Chapter 9: Prenups

The reason you buy car insurance is to protect yourself in case an accident happens but buying car insurance doesn't mean you're planning to get into an accident. Much like getting a pre-nuptial agreement doesn't mean you're planning for divorce. Like car accidents, divorce happens, so why not protect yourself from that like you would your car? Comedian Tony Rock said, "I'm not preparing for my divorce, but if I get divorced, I'm prepared." I polled some of my friends, asking them would they get a pre-nuptial agreement and why. From their answers, I could tell they didn't really know how they worked outside of their mischaracterization in TV & movies. Prenups protect both parties in the case of divorce, and I know you've heard the statistic that fifty percent of marriages end in divorce but not only that, they end in divorce in less than 10 years. The probability of you getting divorced is a coin flip. So, either I'm getting divorced, or you are.

I think the main reason why they are so unpopular is because of how they are portrayed in the media. Because of that, society thinks one way about them, which influences your social circles. "You know she signed a prenup right, couldn't be me." Signing a prenup has always been portrayed as if in a divorce, the woman is left with nothing, and that's not true. Prenuptial agreements must be fair, so he or she can't just leave you with nothing because you will both have separate lawyers working in your best interest. Children from previous relationships are also financially protected by a prenup. This is important because it protects against divorce, where your assets or inheritance will be safe from alimony payments. Furthermore, if you die and don't have a will or will be challenged, the prenup will help divide your assets up and is another form of protection. A prenup can also be changed, so if you'd want your assets divided up differently before, that is possible.

What did Kanye say? "Because when she leave yo ass, she gone leave with half." Half of what? It's commonly understood that one party would take half of your money or assets, but what about half your debt? Yes, that can happen. Say your spouse goes back to school to get a degree and takes out a few student loans that can be considered joint debt because the household in total benefits, not just your spouse, so you can be on the hook for that too in a divorce. What about if your spouse has a secret credit card and has an outstanding balance you don't know about? You can still be on the hook for that regardless of your knowledge of it. Furthermore, say your spouse's investment takes a turn for the worse and now is in debt and you want a divorce, you can still be on the hook for that without a prenup. This isn't an exhaustive list of ways you can incur debt in the instance of a divorce, but I want to make it clear how you might be leaving with half of something you don't want. The state in which you live will determine certain laws and regulations, so it's good to be mindful of that if you decide on a prenup or not.

A prenup is just a safety net and will alleviate lawyers and the court getting too involved in your money. You don't want to harm the person you've been with for a long time just because a marriage didn't work out. Like I said earlier; statistically, the chances of you staying married aren't great, and we all know people who have been married then divorced. Whether it's 2 years or 20 years, do you really want the reason you stay married to me just because you don't want to fork over alimony? "It's cheaper to keep her/him" shouldn't be a reason you stay in an unfavorable marriage.

Again, I think the mindset around prenups needs to change before we start having real conversations about it. Traditionally, when we think of prenups, the woman is usually the damsel in distress where the husband left her with nothing, then he's with his new younger wife on a yacht in San Tropez. She'd be embarrassed to sign one because of how society looks at them, but society is financially illiterate. You're really going to care about the opinions of people who use GoFundMe as a life insurance policy? People's opinions shouldn't matter when it comes to financial protection, especially when their marriage is probably on the rocks too. You're worried about their opinion for no reason other than your own ego. The other thing we are missing is that women are making great strides financially in careers and entrepreneurship. Women should be protected too; this isn't the 60s anymore, and women are now financial powerhouses. They also need protection, and I am sure none of you ladies want to look like Teri Joseph in Soul Food paying her ex-husband alimony.

Chapter 10: Credit Cards

Cut them up. Cut all of them up. Cut up the one for emergencies too. Don't forget that last one. Credit cards are the most predatory financial instrument known to date. These companies literally prey on your ignorance and market to you and offer you 20% off when you open a credit card or 60,000 points when you spend $3,000 in the first three or four months or my favorite, no interest for eighteen months. This is not designed to "reward" you. It's for you to spend more money, which you will do, and then they will benefit from the interest they earn when you don't pay the full statement balance. If you own a credit card, I'm sure you've seen how little the minimum payment is relative to your statement balance. That is by design. Their job is to keep you a customer or in debt for as long as they can for as much interest as the market will bear. Speaking of interest, I bet you don't know your annual interest rate on your credit cards. The point is, you are not smarter than the credit card company because if you were, then the average credit card debt in America wouldn't be $10,000. The techniques they use in marketing and promotions are designed for them to profit off you. Even if you pay your cards off on time every month, statistically, you spend more money using a credit card than you would with cash. The logic behind using cash activates the pain center in the brain that a credit card or debit card does not. When you buy something with cash, it's a visible exchange of physical cash for a good or service. With a credit or debit card, you get your card back; then you get the good you purchased, so there is no visible exchange on your part. You are not winning despite what you think. Why do you think every department store has it? They are cash cows, and all you got was 20% off once.

With all that being said, I LOVE credit cards. I frequently travel, so I have a travel credit card that gets airline miles and points worth 1.5x cash, so it's pretty great for me, and they have many other benefits that I think are worth it. Each credit card has different attributes that make it special such as the double airline miles or two points for every dollar spent on certain companies or industries. They also offer certain levels of consumer protection. It's a level of record-keeping as you know what you spent and when.

With cash, you don't really get that unless you manually do it. They're very convenient, especially in the age where Amazon is king, and everything is more online than traditional brick and mortar stores. Then you have apps like Uber, Postmates, and Zipcar that don't even allow cash, so credit cards are becoming more and more necessary. Finally, they can help build your credit score if you pay on time and frequently, and there are tricks to have payments count twice and so forth and so on, but they can also hurt if you don't pay them on time and accrue credit card debt which is considered bad debt.

I look at credit cards like fire. They can keep your house warm or burn it down. Despite the benefits of credit cards, they are not for everyone. They're not for anyone because they are predatory instruments meant to increase your spending and try to get you to pay interest. But they're okay if you use them right, but it really depends on your mindset. You really need to have an honest conversation with yourself. If you have lingering credit card debt or struggle to make payments or rely on credit because you don't want to pay for something immediately, then credit cards might not be for you, and you should cut them up. If a credit card is used for emergencies, they are also not for you because you don't have the cash to cover an emergency. Debit cards can be good, but they don't have any benefits, and they still make you spend more money, but at least you're not spending money that isn't yours.

We were all young and might've had parents who got us a credit card that was only for gas that ended up being used for food and then eating out and other frivolous purchases. When you were in college, you needed a new outfit and opened that Victoria Secrets credit card and would pay it later, and it's still later, and the interest has equaled the original amount on the card in the first place. We've all been there in some form. Debt snowballing is the best option where you pay the smallest debt first and work up to the larger ones where you pay the minimum amount on the larger ones and put extra on the smaller ones and just keep working your way up. I'll talk about credit coaching in a later chapter because you can do it yourself, but it's kind of like fixing your car, it's possible, but it's probably best to pay a mechanic.

As I said, it's hard to get out of the plastic mindset when we're in an age where cash is becoming obsolete, and credit/debit is simply more convenient, especially now where we can even use our phones to pay for things. While it's more convenient, you're still spending more on average, so try to use the cash more often. I never used to carry cash and barely had cash, but lately, I've been using cash purposely to get out of that mindset, and you can do the same. I'm still pragmatic about where we are in terms of technology, but to curb spending habits and know how much money I started within my wallet and how much I ended with changes my perception of my spending habits.

Chapter 11: Credit Repair

When you think of a credit score, good or bad, what do you think that means? It doesn't have anything to do with how much money you have or make. It's more about how good or bad you are at borrowing money. I have an 800 FICO score. This means that I am very good at using other people's money to buy things. While that's a bit exaggerated, it is mostly true. If you think about it if you don't pay your credit card, which is debt, what happens to your credit score? It goes down. If you use cash or debit, your credit score does nothing. When you think about it like that, you can understand what a credit score means because I feel like we've glorified it, but essentially, it's an indicator of how good or bad you are at buying things you can't afford. I am not saying having a good credit score isn't necessary because it is. Some jobs won't hire you if you have bad credit. What I am saying is what your credit score represents is indicative of a bigger problem.

Of course, you're not here for my perspective, and you're here for the how do I fix this. The first step in improving your credit to understand how you got here. Whether your mother put a bill in your name when you were young, or you made some bad decisions as a teenager, or medical bills have gotten the best of you. As crazy as it sounds, some have experienced all three. Once you've figured out how you got there, you know what not to do again. Luckily, there are many free tools to help fix it, but it will take some work. The first free tool is the Internet. We live in a time when knowledge is at our fingertips as to what ways to go and understand how credit and debt work. Understanding that all debt is not viewed as equal will help you make better financial choices in debt. For example, a $20,000 car loan, a depreciating asset, is considered bad debt. In comparison, a $20,000 student loan is deemed to be good debt as this has the chance to increase your net worth.

Ordering your credit report is of the utmost importance. The main reason is that chances are, you've never done it. When you do it, you'll understand why. Your credit report will contain quite a few errors, even silly errors. Your name or birthday might be incorrect. These are the simple things that should be right, so if these credit bureaus can't even spell your name right, then you know that they're not reporting your credit history correctly. You are responsible for your financial life, so act like it because they don't care about your credit score like you do. They're not the ones who can't get a loan at a decent interest rate; you are. You are allowed one free credit report a year, and you can get that from myfreecreditreport.com. While you're at it, order a credit report for everyone in your house. It will need some personal information, so explain what you're doing and have them give you the information. It's a simple and straightforward website that will mail you a copy of your credit report from all three credit bureaus: Experian, Equifax, and Transunion. After ordering, you can start looking through it and making sure everything is accurate. There might be an account opened that you don't recognize or something you thought you paid off that is being reported as not paid. After you find all the incorrect information, it's time to get on the phone with these credit bureaus to rectify the misinformation. While the three credit bureaus can help you with incorrect marks against you, there probably will be marks that are true as well. In this case, you have to contact the lender to discuss any derogatory marks that are true and be very nice to whoever you talk to. They might still say no and leave a mark on there, but you won't know until you ask. This is controversial, but you can elect to dispute every accurate derogatory mark on your credit reports too. When you dispute a derogatory mark on your credit report, the credit bureau will contact the lender to verify the information. If that lender does not respond, the derogatory mark will be wiped away. Marks on your credit report can stay for up to 7 years. That is why it is well worth it to investigate those marks.

Your credit utilization ratio is a determinant of your credit score as well. This means the amount of available credit versus the amount of credit you use can have a sizable impact on your score. Anything over around thirty percent has the chance to impact your score. Let's say you have $100,000 of available credit and you're $70,000 in debt. That is 70% credit utilization, which is terrible. If you increase your credit limits, you'll have more available credit if you don't use the increased credit amount. So, if you increase your credit limit from $100,000 to $130,000 and you're $70,000 in debt, then your ratio drops to 54%, which isn't good, but your credit score will increase as well as you're still paying on it. This is simple to do, you'll get offers to do it, but you can also ask creditors to increase your credit limit. Again, do not use the extra credit.

When you pay off one bill or credit card, pat yourself on the back because now, you can save whatever money you were paying on that. Wrong. What you want to do is use whatever amount you paid monthly or weekly to the debt you just closed and add that amount to another payment. This is what we call debt snowballing. For example, if you paid $200 a month on your Visa and a $500 a month payment on an AmEx card, you're paying $700 a month total. Say you pay off the Visa, then you apply the $200 you were paying to the $500 payment you're still paying on your AmEx, so now you're paying $700 on the AmEx, and once that's finished applying the $700 to another credit card loan or bill. The trick is to start paying off small bills and work your way up to larger ones. This will help you quickly eliminate debt, decrease your credit utilization, and in turn, increase your credit score. Remember never to close a credit card when you pay it off. This will only help you because of the length of your credit history. When your credit is pulled, your credit score will take a small hit. For loans or credit cards or renting an apartment, this is common that the lender will do what's called a hard pull or hard inquiry on your credit, so you want to have as few of those as possible over a certain period. Becoming an authorized user on a close friend or family member's credit card will boost your score as you get the benefits of their good credit habits. They can elect to give you a credit card or not, but either way, you'll benefit from their credit habits, which will boost you up some points. There are drawbacks to this, however. If they have a lot of debt on that card, that will not benefit you, and if they miss payments or anything like that, your credit score will be hurt. Essentially, you're bonded in a way, so only do this with someone you know is reliable. People who'd want to make a friend or family member an authorized user, help them out. Again, you don't have to give them a credit card, so it's just them riding your coattails without the risk of them using your credit.

For those of you with children, if your credit is good, it might be a good idea to put their names on a bill or two to help them get some credit history going and giving them a head start. Parents, this is only recommended if you're good and responsible. Please do not put your children through anything financially when your finances are in shambles. This is a great way to teach your kids about credit as well. There's no need to do it when they're small children or anything; maybe once they get to high school, you can help them get some credit established.

As you can see, fixing your credit on your own isn't too hard. It takes a lot of work, but I know you know it is well worth it. There are plenty of apps, and companies like credit karma and banks are now letting you see your credit score as well, so you can easily track how you're doing. Investing in a credit coach is also a good idea because they will do a lot of work for you. It guarantees you're doing the right thing as opposed to you thinking you're doing the right thing. They can be expensive, but they help you get off to a good start and take it from there.

Chapter 12: Identity Protection

"Identity theft is not a joke, Jim. Millions of families suffer every year." A famous quote by the esteemed Dwight K. Schrute holds and is only becoming a larger problem. Companies who house tons of your data, like Yahoo and Equifax both have had massive data breaches. Hopefully, you were not one of these people, but it was just random bad luck even if you were. This can happen to anyone. Your identity is the most valuable intangible thing you own. Criminals know this, and that is why they are so vigilant. Criminals need only a few items of information to effectively steal your identity, making it difficult to protect it fully. All they need is your name, where you grew up, college, where you work, and they are good. Essentially, everything on your Facebook or Tinder profile is a wet dream for an identity thief. We unknowingly make it easy for criminals to steal our identity. We don't know how to do our due diligence in protecting ourselves to prevent identity theft or catch identity theft early, so generally, we only find out by mistake. Usually, it's only when we try to get a loan or open a credit card. We are shockingly denied. Do we suspect our identity may have been stolen? Again, don't let it be you because you aren't on top of your finances.

Your credit report should be checked yearly. This is the best way to see any accounts opened that you are not familiar with. The long and short of it is that something can be opened in your name, but you might not get the bill for it, so your credit report is the only way to know. Like I said before, you get one free a year, so it's of zero cost and minimal effort to make sure you're in good shape. Credit freezes are amazing because you can freeze all pulls and inquiries on your credit. When you freeze your credit, creditors will not see your credit report and won't open an account. You see where I'm going with this. This service is free depending on the credit bureau and the state you live in. At most, it cost about $10. It can be a hassle when you are trying to open accounts, but you're not just randomly opening accounts, so it's still worth it. You'll also receive a pin to freeze and unfreeze your credit. It's not a perfect system and can get inconvenient, but it's well worth the hassle to keep your money safe.

Credit monitoring is becoming increasingly popular, especially after the Equifax hack but don't confuse it with credit protection. Credit monitoring only alerts you when changes happen involving your credit. When you open a new account, when your credit score changes and things like that, it's more of an alert than a preventive measure. Think of it as a home security system. It is still beneficial because it's active ongoing protection as opposed to an annual credit report, so if you check your credit report, then six months later someone opens an account in your name, you'll get a notification as opposed to having to wait six months before you realize it's on your credit report. I have one of these resources, which I pay for through my job. It monitors many key points in your life, from your credit data to your social media. It also keeps track of your digital exposure, which pops up when you search your name on Google. It keeps track of all your information, from your name to your jobs, etc. It's interesting when you look at all the info about your life archived on the Internet. You can customize it to display whatever information you like, specifically whatever information you like monitored.

Since everything is online and digital, it's more avenues to get your data, but you can do a few more practical things. Since most of the day we're on the Internet, you should only use sites with the padlock icon before the URL. This identifies the site as safe and secure instead of a sketchier website, which might have less protection of your data. Using difficult passwords and changing your password every month or so should be a given as well. I understand it's very inconvenient as we all have a million passwords. Still, your phone does a good job of making it a little easier. Your purses and wallets are potentially vulnerable as everything uses an RFID chip. It can be intercepted through technology that will copy your credit cards and then have your card information. Companies are now lining wallets and purses with a material that block that from happening. In a pinch, you can just use aluminum foil.

One day, I got a phone call saying that the IRS was investigating me, and I had to call this number before legal action was taken against me. I called them, and they were asking for my social security number to "verify" me, and that's when I knew it was a scam. It's plenty of scams that get access to your phone number, and nobody legitimate will call you and ask for your social or bank password. If you are ever a victim of identity fraud, it is a world of hell, so just be safe and put a condom on your identity.

Chapter 13: Will

It's not fun to think about your death but guess what, the grim reaper does not care. Generally, you don't need a will if you don't have a positive net worth, un-married, and have no children. While that is many people, especially young people, it is still important to have a will. You still have what's called digital assets such as online banking, online investing like an Acorns Digit or Coinbase, as well as your social media profiles, which might have value based on your followers or content. For some of these digital assets, you need a will for someone else to access in the event of your death unless they have a beneficiary option. Cohabitating is becoming more popular amongst millennials, but there is no legal backing because you're essentially roommates. In this case, a will can help you direct assets to that individual because it will default to your next of kin, and you might not want them to have it.

If you die without a will, you died what's called intestate, which means the government must distribute assets based on your state's law. When this happens, assets usually default to your spouse. If you're not married, your children and your parents or other family then go to the state. A will takes care of this in a more directed way. You can direct how much goes to who or what. For example, 50% of the money can go to your children; then the other 50% can go to a charity if you choose to set it up like that.

The traditional way to get a will done is with a lawyer, but you can make one quickly through an online site with more things online. Constructing a will when you have a considerable amount of assets is best done with a lawyer. Still, for those who want something simply because they don't have much, a will you do yourself is enough. They are usually straightforward and walk you through what goes where and then it just must be notarized when you're finished to make it binding. While you might not do a will, anything involving money like investments accounts, 401(k), or banks have something that you can designate whom this money would go to if you do die, so do that at the very least.

Chapter 14: Parents

Since college, I've been working a lot and traveling a lot. I lived in different states and enjoyed living the millennial dream. While I've been living and enjoying my life, my parents have been getting older. I've been very fortunate that my parents are still in good health and active, but father time is undefeated. They'll retire and become increasingly handicapped, as things naturally happen when people get older. I've been fortunate enough to have both of my parents all my life. Those of you who have also been as fortunate need to start having conversations about their more senior life stages. Are they going to live in their house? Is the house paid off? When will the house be paid off? Do they have a will? Power of attorney? Life Insurance? A Living will? Will the need to move in with you? Assisted Living? How much is that? Who's paying for it? How much is in the 401(k)? How much is in savings? Will they want to downsize the house? What about your spouses' parents? What if they get sick? Should I start putting money aside? And a lot of other questions that need to be discussed for their wellbeing and yours. You know how your parents are with money, so you have a good idea of how much you might need to step in to help. The last thing you want to have to do is financially support your parents in their twilight. You ideally want them to be safe and financially secure on their own and at peace.

Modern medicine has afforded more people in our society longer lives than ever before. Unfortunately, we are outliving our money, and that's if we had money saved in the first place. Having conversations while your parents are healthy is important not only for their benefit but also for your peace of mind. Seeing your parents deteriorate in life will be difficult. You want your money to help alleviate some of that burden. So, what are you going to do? The bottom line is they're getting older, and so are you. Those senior years are coming, so plan now while time is on you and your parents' side instead of when catastrophe hits and you're playing catch up. The key to finance and life is proactive and not reactive. You will have a ton you need to react to already, so take care of the things you know will happen as quickly as possible.

Chapter 15: Home Buying

Homeownership is considered the epitome of the American dream. It is the best way to create wealth through equity and ownership. While I feel that way, I will give a more pessimistic perspective towards home buying than is often conveyed. To be clear, I am not saying that you shouldn't buy a home because that is what we should strive for and a great wealth-building tool, but these are maybe things you didn't think about.

A lot of times, I hear the phrase "I'm just throwing away money renting." That is an untrue statement. You are not throwing away money or wasting money by renting. Renting is essentially testing your patience and discipline. Think about the things that can be done while you're renting and not bogged down by the debt or responsibility of a house. If you already have $100,000 in student loan debt and/or credit card debt, do you really want to add another pile of debt? The average price of a home in the U.S. is $294,000. Just imagine adding that amount of debt to your life. Renting is debt-free, however, because you don't own the place you're living. Renting is also infinitely more flexible than buying. You can break a lease; you can't break a mortgage. With a lease, you can pay your cancellation fee to break it, or some have clauses if your job moves you a certain distance, it is waived then after that, you are free to go. You don't have to worry about selling it. Imagine trying to sell your house during a financial crisis or a recession because you got a great job opportunity in another state. Still, you can't take it because you bought a house. A mortgage payment can be cheaper than a rent payment but would an air conditioning unit in a place you rent cost more to replace or a place you own? What about when tax payments go up in a place you rent vs. a place you own? More nuanced because when the taxes go up, that is partially offset by your rent payment going up, so you do pay a little of that. The catch is, you can move at the end of your lease and find more competitive pricing if it gets too expensive. Selling a house where taxes or HOA fees are going up more and more, good luck. I would recommend talking to homeowners around your age or a little older, asking people who've paid their homes off or have moved a few times, and ask them what that process is like. They might have a different answer than what you're expecting, and if they don't, then at least you got some perspective.

Buying a multi-family unit and living in one unit and renting it out is another thing I hear a lot. Again, great idea, but you probably don't understand what goes into it if you've never done it. From what I gathered, people think it's as simple as buying a multi-unit building live in one rent out the other two, and the cash flows right. It doesn't miss a beat but being a landlord is still a job. Your tenants might ruin carpet or tile, and you must fix it. If you've lived in an apartment before, then you know things go wrong, so don't expect a smooth ride. You might have to take tenants to court and get lawyers and get tied up in legal fees. You can Google landlord horror stories for days. It might be better ways to invest given your certain situation, which might be the best way to invest and get into real estate. I am simply saying don't expect it to be an easy ride is all.

I'll get off my soapbox now.

Homeownership should be the goal at some point. I am in the process of buying a condo, and it is a lot that goes into it. The first thing to do is to know what you want in a house, condo townhouse, or a multi-unit property. I've been just looking without the help of a realtor for about six months on the home search aggregators like Zillow and Trulia, as well as going to open houses, and I've learned a lot. I know what I do and don't like about certain houses and what I like and don't like in the neighborhoods. I did this without getting a realtor because I felt like that would have accelerated my progress more than I'd like. I do intend to use a realtor, but I'd want to go to him or her with more direction, so that's also why I waited. You might not mind having a fixer-upper. In that case, you want to look at buying the cheapest house in the best neighborhood you can afford, and you can fix it up to your liking. You might also look at buying a foreclosed home, which has pros and cons, but a good realtor can help you navigate this as a viable option. Having a good realtor is paramount. Like any profession, the more years of experience, the more valuable, and that's not necessarily true for finding an agent because you still have to mesh well with them. You have to trust that they are looking out for you and not just trying to make their sale. Luckily everyone knows someone who's purchased a home, so you can consider that agent as well as an agent you might find. A family friend or an agent you met at an open house can be great options as well. You simply want to have plenty of options to find the right agent for your situation.

When you get pre-approved for a loan, you'll notice that they'll approve you for the amount you can spend, but this isn't the amount you can afford. This is just how much the lender will allow you to borrow. If you're buying a house for the amount you're approved for, you're probably making a mistake. There are plenty of affordability calculators you can play around with that will let you enter in variables to see exactly how much you can afford. That number varies depending on what factors you put in, though. Getting pre-qualified and pre-approved are two completely different things. Pre-qualified simply means this is how much you can expect to borrow. Pre-approval will consider a lot more than the pre-qualification. You need to complete a mortgage application and provide pay stubs, W-2 information, and credit scores. It's essentially a background check. After this is done, you will know what interest rate you will pay on the loan. Like most things, you want to shop around for the best rate. You have several loan types to choose from, whether it's FHA or VA, or traditional loans. Each one has specific attributes, which make them viable for your individual situation. FHA loans are for first time home buyers. It's a lower down payment percentage, and not too high of a credit score is needed. One of the main cons of this loan is mortgage insurance, which can't be removed from the loan's life instead of a conventional loan where it can be removed. Though FHA loans are popular amongst new home buyers, you can apply for a conventional loan with a low-down-payment if you have good enough credit. Property mortgage insurance is canceled. Your state housing association might have grant programs for down payments. For some, you must be a first-time homebuyer; you might not have to be a first-time buyer for others. For example, in my state, first-time homebuyers can have $7,500 in down payment assistance if you get a 30-year fixed-rate mortgage and stay in the house for at least five years. If you sell the house before the five-year period, you must pay the grant or part of the grant back. These are great, but if you have good credit and enough for a down payment, be mindful of those loan programs' interest rates. If you get a $7,500 grant at a 4.25% interest rate on a 30-year loan, the PMI that is not cancellable so think long term when taking advantage of these programs. Check to see what home buying programs are available in your state.

When picking your loan, you have a few options on how you want to repay it in the form of a mortgage. You can do a fixed interest loan, which means your interest rate is static through a loan's life instead of a variable loan, which fluctuates with market trends. The one you choose is solely up to how much risk you'd like to take. There are a few other loan types, but those are the most common. The other option you have is how long you want to pay for the home. Generally, 15 or 30 years are the options. The key differences are the amount you pay monthly and the amount of interest you pay for the loan's life. Obviously, the longer you take to pay the loan, the more interest you pay over the life of the loan, so remember that when you think about how much you'll end up paying in total. Regardless of the life of your loan, you can pay a loan off early. If you get an inheritance or a nice bonus at work and you'd like to put that towards your loan amount, you'd want to make sure of two things. One, ensure that lump of money is going toward the loan principal and not the interest. Two, ensure there is no prepayment penalty meaning you aren't penalized for paying your loan early. If you intend to pay your loan off early but will be penalized, putting that money into an investment account is a viable option. If you don't have a prepayment penalty and can pay that loan off early, then that's probably your best bet. Another option is to put the money in an investment account. The rationale is that an investment account could garner higher gains than the interest you'd pay on a loan. In theory, you'd net a positive gain from the interest in the investment account relative to the interest you'd pay on a loan. This sounds good in theory, but if the housing or stock market crashes, then you're in a terrible position.

Title insurance is necessary when buying any type of property. Title insurance protects you from a cloudy title, which might include complications with the deed or if there are liens or levies on the property. The property seller could not be aware of any title issues, as it could have spawned from something they were unaware of when they purchased the property. You will have two title insurance protections. One is a lender's policy, which will protect you if you take out a property loan. This is in effect until you pay off the loan or refinance. The second one is an owner's policy, which for the amount you paid for the home in the case you are sued due to a claim against the home. This is useful for repairs or improvements you might've done that exceed the loan amount. Title insurance is a one-time cost and won't be added to your mortgage. The price will vary depending on several factors. Some insurance is a scam or unnecessary, but this is not one of them. Make sure you get title insurance and protect yourself and your investment.

You might end up paying more than the asking price because you'll be submitting an offer or a bid, which is just like eBay, where you may not be the only bidder interested. You will also be able to put in how much you're willing to go above another offer too. So, if you put in a bid for $150,000 with a max of $175,000 and another offer comes in at $160,000, you can set how much over that offer you'd like to go so it could be $161,000, which would be $1,000 over the other offer but still below your $175,000 max. This is called an escalation clause. The downside of this is that you must disclose how much you're willing to spend on the house to the seller. So, they can bring you closer to their asking price than you possibly would've paid if they didn't know how much you were willing to spend.

Knowing how much you can afford in a mortgage payment helps you understand how not to overspend. Generally, your total monthly mortgage should not exceed more than twenty-eight percent of your pre-tax income. Total housing expenses (mortgage, property tax, insurance, etc.) should not be more than thirty-two percent of your pre-tax income. Finally, the max amount of debt should not exceed forty percent of your pre-tax income. This includes everything from your mortgage to your credit card bill to your car payment. If you are over forty percent of your income in debts already, then a house buying is not for you right now. When saving for a down payment, don't forget about the closing costs and the costs of the appraisal, inspection, lawyers, and earnest money. These are all things that get overlooked when saving to buy a home. You might get grants or credits toward your closing costs or down payment but do not rely on that.

I know I just trashed buying a multi-family unit and renting the vacant units, but that is an amazing way to offset your mortgage payment and possibly produce an income. This is a great way to invest in real estate for anybody but especially first-time homebuyers. Since you're buying anyway, why not buy two, one for you to live in and one to rent out. They're easy to finance because you're eligible for more ways to finance as well as great tax benefits. There are plenty of downsides, however. Since you are the landlord, you are responsible for all maintenance that you will have to outsource to whatever contractor services your needs. The best way to find reliable contractors is through word of mouth because a bad contractor can be as much of a headache as the repair is. You also have to think about your tenants, which you can never fully trust that they'll be perfect. Still, you can pull credit scores background checks and ask for references to better understand who they are as a person and trust your instincts. If you're buying any multi-family home you also intend to live in, be mindful of how much access you want tenants to have to you. If you don't want them to have any direct contact or even know you're the owner, a property manager is worth the investment. Property managers are around 10% of the monthly rental income, and they are precious whether you live in the building or not. Property managers do all the screening of tenants as well as looking for tenants. He or she will also be the tenant's point of contact for things like repairs or inquiries, so they don't even have to know who you are or that you live there. There will be periods where you might go months without a tenant or residual income that you were using to offset your mortgage. That expense will now fall on you because you don't know how long it will take to get another tenant in after the previous tenant moves out. You also don't know how long the until will be out of commission if you must do repairs after they leave. Before you buy, it might be a good idea to find the rental rates, which will detail how much you can reasonably charge for rent. Multi-family units can be hard to find in metro areas, and they're not as plentiful as single-family homes, so you might have to do more work to find one. A good alternative would be buying multi-family units in college towns as college students are always looking for housing.

Have you ever asked yourself why there are so many mattress or furniture stores on the same street? You're probably asking yourself how these furniture and mattress stores all are staying in business, especially being so close to each other. Well, that is because the markup on furniture is extremely high. It's a very profitable business. Due to this extreme mark up, furniture is not cheap, but there are ways to weave around paying full price. Understanding how to procure furniture, whether you buy it or receive it as a gift, is an art. Before you purchase a house, a budget for how much you want to spend on furniture reasonably. I personally feel this is a nuanced answer because the beauty of buying furniture is you don't have to buy everything at once. In my specific situation, I'll be buying everything for the first time. I plan to buy the bed and couch and TV first. Like the dinner table, recliners, and office furniture, everything else can come at another time. It's also important to understand what share of your budget you want to allocate to specific items. For example, the bed and couch are items I'm going to spend much more of my budget on than dining table bar stools.

Buying new isn't always the best idea, depending on your budget. It may be better to buy a used dresser at an estate sale vs. buying a new one at Ikea because it is likely of higher quality and may last longer, which brings me to my next point. The best option for buying furniture is generally not the store. Estate sales, thrift shops, and gifts are great ways to get great furniture for a deal, but it might take a little more legwork. Get out of the idea of thinking about what you want your place to look like before you buy anything, work out what you want your place to look like around the pieces you find. DIY is the closest thing to handiwork that most millennials will get to, and it's a great way to save money and customize pieces you find at garage sales or thrift shops. Say you find a nice table structurally; it has a few dents and dings. A paint job, sanding, or something as simple as adding a tablecloth might make those dents or dings effectively nonexistent. Kind of like how your cell phone might look bad cosmetically; until you put that case on it, then its imperfections aren't even noticeable. I am a big believer in buying things once, even if you might have to pay a little more. It's a lot more of a hassle and cost more sometimes trying to save money by foregoing quality or trends. You want pieces to last long structurally and not look outdated. Avoid items that are stapled or cheap material because it's just not going to last very long. You'll be rebuying it sooner than you want and spending more money than had you just been patient. You get what you pay for most times. Speaking of beds, pillow-top mattresses are great, but the pillow top might not last as long as the mattress. A mattress topper might be a better option instead of buying a pillow top. Trend-proof furniture pieces will also save you a lot of money because once the trend is over and something goes out of style, you'll want to replace it.

When you go to furniture stores, make sure you bring a gun and shoot it in the air a few times and tell them to leave you alone while shopping because the salesperson will annoy you to no end. When you do go, be wary of buying from a store that offers 0% interest even if you intend to use cash because they increase the prices to account for the financing program they have. I don't think you should ever go into debt to buy furniture, but the 0% interest is for a sure scam. It's 0% interest if you meet a certain criterion. The penalty is usually deferred interest, which means if you pay the loan in the time frame they specify in the terms, you're fine. If you don't, you will pay all the interest you would've paid if you didn't have zero percent interest. This is what I mean by positioned to fail.

This is not the case normally as people have had houses or apartments before and will be carrying over some things to the new place. A bed or a couch or something, maybe everything, but you're moving into a new space, so I think it's unlikely you don't buy at least a few new things. Estate sales, garage sales, consignment, and outlet stores are great ways to get good deals on furniture.

Chapter 16: Cars

I have a question for you. What is your car doing right now? When you go to work, what is your car doing while you're at work? When you get home and go to bed, what is your car doing? It's just sitting there. Throughout the life of your car, you will only use it four percent of the time. So, paying for 100% of the car note, repairs, and insurance and using it four percent of the time. A car is a costly consumer good that also depreciates significantly. The average cost of a monthly car payment in the US is $530, not including insurance. We can say a modest $125 for that; you're paying $655 for something you use four percent of the time. Then you have four oil changes, one repair over $500, a traffic ticket, maybe an accident, and don't forget gas. All of that for something, you use four percent of the time. That is debt and draining your money that could be used for something else. Imagine putting that same $655 a month away for a year. You'd have $7,860 saved up. Do you have a years' worth of car payments and insurance in your savings account right now? Go to page 96 and do the exercise below to see how much you're paying yearly and how much value you're getting relative to the cost of owning a vehicle.

To my fellow millennials, stop buying these expensive ass cars you can't afford, and you know you can't afford just because the car dealership makes the monthly payments look manageable. With any car loan over five years, you got screwed over, and you know it. Still, you wanted to get your payments down to be able to afford this S class BMW that your parents had to co-sign for you to have a $620 car note over six years. Let me guess, you cracked $60,000 at your job, and you said let me get a Mercedes or an Audi. For what? Is that the best use of your money? If you have life and disability insurance outside of your job, a 401(k) or IRA saving at least 15%, an emergency fund, and your loans paid off, and drive a luxury car that you paid in cash, then ill shut up. I know that it is unlikely for someone under 30 years old to have all those things to buy luxury cars. Not only are you paying for the car note, but repairs and gas are much higher. Not to mention car insurance is higher. It's just not the best use of your money even if you can afford it. I would love someone to argue against what I'm saying here because I just don't see it.

To be completely honest, I am 100% against cars, new or used. They depreciate significantly; you only use them four percent of the time, car insurance, repairs, the risk of an accident or the car breaking down, the price of gas, parking, city stickers, state property taxes, and many other reasons. It's just not economical or practical. I'm in the process of exploring moving to a more metro area where a car isn't as necessary, especially with Uber, Lyft, Zipcar, turo, trains and buses, and a lot of other modes of transportation. Even grocery shopping and food delivery are possible. I think ridesharing is the infant stage of what automated cars look like where people don't own cars but own a subscription service. This way, there are fewer cars on the in-production, which is great for the planet and great for traffic and eliminates the need for all the tedious activities associated with owning a car. It's a lot safer, in theory. The next time you drive in a big city, see how many cars you see parked on the street. That could be eliminated when automated cars become more prevalent because people won't own cars, so no need to park because it would work like uber where you get to your destination and the cargoes and picks someone else up, and then a car comes and gets you when it's time for you to go. The amazon delivery of uber eats and post mates will only get bigger and more efficient, further limiting the need for a car. The only reason I could see the need for a car now is if you live in an area where rideshare or on-demand services are nonexistent or limited or have small children. If we could get away from car ownership, all the cons of a car in terms of depreciation, high car notes, and the responsibility of owning a car goes away for a more efficient system.

A car is a large time commitment. An oil change takes about an hour of your day, and they always find something else you need to be repaired. Then you need a vehicle emissions test, which is very infrequent and not a big deal unless you don't pass. The DMV for anything is always a hassle because they're open when most people are at work, and then you have to go on a Saturday and wait in line. A car accident is a big-time commitment – find a shop to get it fixed, then deal with the insurance company that might try to shaft you on a technicality. Even if everything goes well, you're out of your car for a while, depending on how severe the damage is. When those red and blue lights flash behind you, your anxiety goes through the roof as you don't know what you're in for, whether it's an unpleasant experience that results in a ticket or you're being taken in for the suspended license you had no idea about. Then, taking time off from work in court to get your license back and pay the ticket's cost. A DUI is no joke either, or for those of you that might have one, uber is your only option depending on your situation. Even buying a car is terrible. Given all the risks associated, owning a car really isn't worth it, especially a brand new one. I would argue that using ridesharing services is effectively cheaper and much less time consuming than owning a car and especially owning a car you're paying a loan on. I tell people if you're monthly rideshare bill is the same as your monthly car note. Ridesharing is still cheaper because you're not paying insurance, you're not paying gas, you're not accountable for depreciation, you're not paying for repairs yearly registration or city stickers, and most of all, you have peace of mind that if something goes wrong, it is not your problem because it is not your car. Every day on my commute to work, I see at least one accident, or one car pulled over to the side, or someone stopped by the police. I do not want those problems anymore, and hopefully, you don't either.

Leasing versus buying confounds most car buyers, and no one really understands what leasing a car means. People just know the payments are cheaper, but they're cheaper for a reason. When you lease a car, you're paying for the depreciation, so they've calculated how much the car will be worth at the end of the lease. Not to mention the money factor which is similar to an interest rate for a loan.

I feel like leasing is really for the rich because it's a terrible method to procure a car. I guess the only good thing about leasing is that you don't own it. It's only for a finite period with a mile restriction, so you're giving the car back. Still, you have to buy another car which another down payment unless your dealership will let you lease without another down payment because you're buying the same make. One con that most people don't think about is your down payment can be lost if you total your car relatively soon after you buy it; the insurance company won't reimburse you for your down payment, so that is lost money. Remember, you still have to put a down payment on the car lease, but since you're not buying the car, the money would be lost in the event of an accident that totals your car. If you're leasing a car because the payments would be lower or more affordable, you can't afford the car or the lease. I'm talking to you, millennials. When I did this, I leased my car and then bought it two years later because I started doing Uber and was relocating. Still, it made sense to buy it from the beginning in hindsight because now I'd be done paying or at least closer to paying off the car. Now I'm trying to pay it off, so I can sell it and be completely car-free. My argument against it is that if you only want to have a car for a finite amount of time like if you live somewhere where you need a car but plan to relocate, leasing would be an argument. But you could save a lot of money and get something cheaper. With the down payment and maybe a little more, you can buy something modest own the car, have no car payments, and when you're done with it, then you can just sell it. With a lease, you just borrow the car for a lot of money and then give it back.

When buying a car, you have a lot more to consider. Before you step into the dealership, you have some prep work to do. First, you see how much you can afford, which is different for everyone, but a general rule is 35% of your income. After that, you have to pick a car you want. Sundays are the best days to go to the dealership to look because car dealerships are closed so that you can look in the lot hassle-free. After you've found a car, look at the sticker price, then go to TrueCar to find the value of the car you're interested in. TrueCar is essentially a database of sale prices in your local area, giving you an idea of how many other customers who bought that same car paid for it. It'll tell you the sticker price and then the average amount of savings off the sticker price and then a TrueCar price, which is the customers' price. TrueCar also helps you identify which types of rebates or incentives you might be eligible for. These can range from a military rebate or a recent grad rebate, or the car company might have some rebates. This is not an exhaustive list, so still do your research on if you're eligible for any others. The car salesman might notify you of some because that increases the chances of the car being sold. A friend I consulted for this book used to be a car salesman. I've known him for over ten years, and he's a genuine guy and sounds trustworthy, so his skills translate well into car sales. A lot of car sales associates are like that, but it is all a ploy. Never trust the car salesperson. He or she is out for his interest and the interest of the dealership alone. They will put you in a six-year loan with no money down with the add ons and an extended warranty knowing you can't afford it and not lose any sleep over it. That is the name of the business. There are some things you can do to protect yourself, however. Always put money down. Obviously, the more money you put down, the better but at least enough equivalent to the car's taxes. There are a few reasons why you want to put as much down as possible. First, cars, especially newer cars, depreciate at an extreme rate, so buying a car with little or no money down almost guarantees you'll be upside down on your car because your monthly payment likely won't keep up with the depreciation of the car. The salesperson also isn't going to tell you how much the car depreciates over time. After the first year, the car will depreciate up to twenty percent and up to around ten percent annually until year five. I didn't even factor in the depreciation you're going to get from the miles you put on the car or an accident. You can see that buying a five-year-old car is the best way to avoid significant depreciation. So, whatever car you're looking at buying, look at the model from five years ago and see how much that model depreciated. Never finance a car through a dealership; always find your own financing through either a bank or a credit union. They essentially work the same, but when the dealership does it, the operate on your behalf to find financing for you, which can take a lot of pulls on your credit, which will lower your credit score as well as they can give you a higher interest rate than the bank approved you for to make the difference as a commission. Another thing car salesman will do is have you fill out a referral sheet. They will say this is to give them a reference to reach out to see if they're interested in buying a car but ill discuss what it's really for in a second. Credit and income are king. Obviously, the better your credit, the more likely they'll be able to find you financing, and of course, your income determines what you can afford. The salesman will take your numbers to their desk manager to see what they can do for your situation and do one of three things. First, if you had a car in mind that your income and credit won't support, they will steer you to another car more in your range. The second thing they will do if your credit and income are both bad; they will get you out of the dealership because it's nothing they can do for you. Now, if your credit is bad or you don't have any credit history, then they'll ask you for a co-signer to get you a better interest rate. Let's say you don't have anyone in mind that would co-sign for you. Remember that "reference sheet" of names you filled out earlier? That's what that is for. Not only that, but these companies also want their money and want some people who might know your whereabouts if you start getting behind on your payments, and the repo man must get involved. Again, these salesmen are not your friends.

When you trade-in your car, you're probably getting scammed. Chances are, you are upside down on your auto loan, but you get a call from the dealership saying, "how would you like to upgrade to a new car? We can keep you around the same amount you're paying". When you do this and owe more than the car is worth, you have to roll what's called negative equity into the new car loan to make your payments either higher or extend the original loan's length.

Say you owe $10,000 on your car loan and the car is only worth $6,000, then you have $4,000 of negative equity. So, they will roll that $4,000 of negative equity into your new car loan. You are better off paying off the car and selling it yourself. The dealership will screw you. You can look up your Kelly Blue Book value and go around that price instead of trusting a dealership. The only time a trade-in would make sense is if you're not upside down on the car.

Buying a car is kind of like a jigsaw puzzle where each payment is a piece of that puzzle. You see the car's price when you buy, which is the picture on the box, so you know what it looks like at the end, but you focus on the pieces instead of the big picture, and that's how they get you. The same car can have a different payment amount, but it's still the same price at the end, except you're paying more or less in interest. When I was buying my car, we got to the price, and they weren't telling me how much the total car would be; they were telling me how much the monthly payments would be. If you're not me, you're not busting out the calculator and doing that math to say okay at this interest rate. This is how much the total car will cost, which is how much value it will have when making payments. You're not doing that, and the salesman is not doing that for you because they know big numbers scare people.

The sticker price is the main thing people pay attention to because it's the most expensive but maybe not the most important thing. I wish it were required to detail how much repairs and maintenance generally cost and the car's price. Obviously, parts for a Toyota Camry will be less expensive than an Audi A7, but those are things they don't tell you to look at, so you have to do some due diligence to see. Even though I know you probably have your heart set on a certain car, take a step outside of yourself and think about how much you would pay for insurance. Extended warranties and add on warranties like wheel and tire insurance are a good idea and might not be necessary. It's debatable whether you need tire dent and ding protection because the money you're spending on the policy could be set to the side on the chance something does happen. For example, if you pay $50 a month for dent and ding protection, you could put that aside instead and have the money for it if something does happen. So, it's just your perspective on which you think is best. That goes for extended warranties as well. Pretty much any time you're getting marketed heavily on something, it's a bad idea. Companies won't market something to you heavily unless they're making a killing on the margins.

If I told you the car's monthly price could either be $350 or $641, which one would you choose, the cheaper one of course. What if I said you could pay your car off in three years or six years? Which one would you choose, the faster one? Well, you can't have the cheaper monthly car price and pay it off faster at the same time. You must pick one slow and cheap or fast and expensive. The catch is, whether you pick the slow and cheap or the fast and expensive route, you're still paying the same $21,000 because it's the same car. Now let's add some interest. Let's add 6.25% interest into this equation. With the slow a cheap method, you're paying $4,237 in interest, and with the fast and expensive method, you're paying $2,084 in interest. That's a little under $2,200 difference in just interest. All because you got a car you can't afford. Now let me ask the question again would you do the slow and cheap method or the fast and expensive method? You chose the slow and cheap method still because you're 24 years old, and this is your dream car for some reason. Millennials, I'm shaking my head at you.

I know this will be unpopular, but if you can't buy a car outright in cash, you shouldn't buy that car. The amount you put on a down payment could buy you a car outright, but "The Jones'" remember. Got to get something nice right. You can't have your friends judging you because you think at your age this is the range of car that's acceptable. I understand. I get it. Go ahead, be in some debt, potentially go upside down or default on your loan because you bought too much car. It happens more than you think. Nobody is broadcasting his or her failures. You know who it doesn't happen to, though, people who buy cars outright. You don't even have to stay in the car long. You can stay in a car for a couple of years, save up more for the next one, and buy that one with the money you saved up. Trade-in your current car for a better car. In that time, you're paying zero interest, you don't have a monthly payment, and you're not locked into the car's loan. So, if something happens then, you're not tied to it. After saying all of that, why would you get a car you can't afford outright? Not to mention the hit to your credit score because you have debt on a depreciating asset. Make the argument, please. I'm all ears.

For some reason, gap insurance isn't as common as it should be, but I feel it's an absolute must-have. Gap insurance protects you from your car being totaled. If you get into an accident and the car is deemed totaled, your insurance company will cut your lender a check for the car's current value. The problem there is if you owe more money than your car is worth, then you have to come up with the remainder of the money to satisfy the loan, so you could be in a position where you have no car, but you still have car payments due to the loan. To avoid this, you get gap insurance. Gap insurance is offered at the dealership, but you can also get it through your personal insurance company, which might be cheaper. Again, if you buy your car outright, this doesn't matter because you don't have a loan.

For rideshare drivers, getting an add on to your insurance policy is of the utmost importance. Rideshare companies offer insurance, but the coverage amounts aren't as strong as traditional insurance because the deductibles are relatively high. When I write this, Lyft's deductible is $2,500, and Uber's is $1,000.

From a rideshare perspective, there are three stages to a pickup. The first stage is idle or roaming time, where you're online waiting for a request. The second stage is when you've accepted a request, and you are in route to that request. The third stage is when the rider is in your car and the trip has started. Rideshare companies don't fully cover you for the first stage. That is when it is expected you go through your traditional insurance company. The second and third stages are when you have more coverage with uninsured and underinsured and comp and collision. If you make a claim, Uber will have you go through your personal insurance first. If they don't cover all of it or deny the claim, then you will go through whichever rideshare platform you were using for coverage. Insurance companies frown upon ridesharing or using your car for anything other than personal use. If you lie and say you weren't when you were, you are committing insurance fraud. Your insurance company will drop you and blacklist you if they find out you are using your vehicle for livery without their knowledge. Rideshare insurance or a commercial auto policy, depending on state laws, will cover you with full coverage in stage one but stages two and three are still through whatever company you are working for. And anything they don't cover, your personal policy with a rideshare endorsement or commercial policy will cover the rest. Rideshare insurance's two main benefits are full coverage for all three stages and avoiding getting blacklisted or dropped from your insurance company. A rideshare endorsement will pay the difference between the deductibles as well. For example, if you have a $500 deductible through your personal policy but file a claim through Lyft, which has a $2,500 deductible, your personal policy with the rideshare endorsement will cover the $2,000 difference between your personal policy deductible and Lyft's deductible. Overall, not having a rideshare endorsement or a commercial policy is very risky. You can Google plenty of stories of rideshare drivers who got into accidents and were out of a lot of money. Don't let it happen to you.

Chapter 17: Traveling

When I was younger, my parents never went anywhere, so neither did I. It never bothered me. Still, it had some effect on me because I travel as much as humanly and financially possible in my adult years. Unfortunately, traveling is an expensive hobby, so I always look for the best ways to save money on hotels, flights, and activities. If you travel a lot or a few times a year, TSA pre-check is a must-have. It's a separate and much shorter security line. And you can keep on your shoes. The longest I've waited to get through security since I've gotten pre-check is ten minutes. The best part is, it's not expensive. It's just $85, and it's good for five years. For an extra $15, you can get what's called global entry that is pre-check for international travel so going through customs is less of a burden.

Travel credit cards are also great, but you must be careful because credit cards are predatory, so everything I said in my credit card chapter applies. With my travel credit card, I get free TSA-Precheck, travel credit, and points that are worth more when you book flights, cars, or hotels through my bank's booking system. It also has certain protections around flight interruption or cancellation. For example, after a trip is delayed more than six hours or is canceled, I can stay in a hotel and eat up to a certain amount on the credit card company's dime. One day my flight got canceled, and I stayed in a close hotel and ate for free. I was only thirty minutes away from home too. One of my favorite perks is lounge access. The lounges are much more comfortable and less crowded in the airports than waiting for a flight or on a layover than with the general population. Some lounges have food and showers, and it's much cleaner. I had a three-hour layover once, and that lounge access came in handy. You don't have to have a travel credit card to get access. However, you can either buy a lounge access card through a priority pass or another company. Some airlines have their own lounges that you can access through a certain status with that airline.

It's quite a few ways to find flights and hotels for a good price. For flights, Google flights is good because you can see the prices for every date and can track flights and searches for price increases and decreases. I also like Hopper, an app that analyzes trends to tell you the best time to buy a flight. It takes the guessing out of picking the right time to buy a flight, so you're not fiddling with buying between Sunday at 7 am or those common tropes that make the news every few years. If you're okay with living on the risky side, there is a website called Skiplagged that will find you flights that indirectly go to your destination, which can be cheaper. For example, if you're flying from Chicago to Las Vegas, Skiplagged will find a flight where the layover in Las Vegas, which is where you're going, but the final destination might be Los Angeles or something like that. This isn't illegal, but it is frowned upon. It can also get tricky if they make you check your bag and don't let you get it back at the layover. I think the safest option is to have a backpack as opposed to a carry-on to avoid this. More importantly, if you have a flight that goes international before it goes to a domestic destination, you will need your passport, or you're in for a hassle. For hotels, I use a combination of a few sites to find the best price. Expedia is good to see all prices. I like Hotwire, which lets you search for hotels at a discount, but the catch is you won't know what hotel you're staying in until you purchase. You can still filter for just the types of hotels you like, say 3 or 4-star hotels only. In the general area as well, you won't know the exact hotel or the exact location.

Saving for trips should always be something you do, no matter how large or small. You'll have a general idea of how much the flights and hotels are. Still, the big variables are activities, transportation, and unexpected costs. Saving up for a trip essentially can be your budget, so anything over the amount you saved up is going above your budget. And if you stay under your budget, it's a plus. If you gamble and make money, then even more of a plus but budget for a loss. For group trips, there should still be a budget of how much spending money everyone needs. This gives everyone a goal to save for this group trip and create a budget for the group. Most people don't think about this, but you should get out of the mindset of individual spending on group trips and start thinking about how much your entire party is spending. Say you and five friends are going on a trip to Miami from Chicago, and flights are, let's say, $350 per person. In total, you all are spending $2,100 to travel when you could severely decrease that amount by renting an SUV and driving to Miami instead. Always think about how much the group is spending for something as opposed to individually. When you have this mindset, sometimes you can pool together and get something better than what it would've cost had you individually made your own way. It's not always feasible but just think through what could be before making a purchase. Realizing your purchasing power as a group makes everyone's money go further.

Never buy a time-share. I'm not even going to go into why just don't do it. Enjoy the benefits of sitting through a presentation because I sure have but never buy one.

Chapter 18: Struggling Family

Parents, siblings, or extended family members that treat us like cash cows. The parents that charged us to rent when they didn't need it or did need it because of their poor financial decisions and masked it with "teaching responsibility." I hear horror stories about kids just graduating college, trying to get their finances together to find a job, and are trying to move out, save money, enjoy the fruits of their labor and do better for themselves but can't because they need to help the family with bills and even the mortgage. Some of us became the breadwinners and the highest educated people in our families, which ironically came with more cost than just being average. Now, I am not against helping around the house or helping through tough times, even contributing to bills groceries here and there. And doing chores, especially if you're getting free lodging because it's only right. You're a non-disabled individual, so you should question the reason why you're expected to contribute financially. Is it because mom and/or dad made some poor decisions? Did they fall on hard times, and it's temporary? Or do they not need the money at all, but they're trying to teach you how to be a man or a woman or whatever B.S. they call it? Then ask yourself, how is this impacting you? When you're the most financially conscious person in the house, it's your responsibility to take control of everyone's finances. This conversation can be tough because you're still their child, and they may still see you as such. But this is something you have to stand your ground on. I don't think it's anything wrong with having full authority over your money and making your parents understand that. Essentially, someone will resent someone in this situation, but one of those scenarios will cost you more money. When you're in situations like this, you're not helping; you're bankrolling their lifestyle, which is full of bad decisions.

Depending on your situation, it might be a good idea to keep your salary to yourself or lie, and while that might be deceitful, it might be for the best. If you make $60,000 as a salary, that's how much other people see. They don't think about the taxes, 401(k), health insurance, student loans, and your bills. They see the $60,000, not the net amount, so they think you make more than you do. Again, they don't care. They see it as more money, and more than likely, you're going to help, so the question becomes how. What I would do is put my foot down and say I'm not helping unless I'm in control of everything. Their way has gotten you all into this cycle, so they don't get to lead anymore.

It's a lot of work to revamp someone else's finances, but since you have to help, now it's your lifestyle too. You have to fix this for everyone. I would start with finding out how much money comes into the house, bills, and expenses and starts a budget. Once you start on a budget, you can see what you can cut out. In my experience, the first thing is cutting up the credit cards, then lowering the cable and cell phone bills. An antenna and Netflix can replace cable television. The phone bill can probably be reduced if you do a little magic and limit the data plans. You don't need that much of a data plan nowadays because everywhere has Wi-Fi. Get creative; you might even have to start handing out allowances. Now, this is not a one-size-fits-all answer, and it will take more tact than I might've given. So be kind but stern, as this could be a potentially big lifestyle change for your family. No one likes to feel dumb, and no one thinks they're bad with money. Hence, stubbornness is likely to be associated with that tough conversation. This lifestyle might be a cycle they're simply repeating. Their parents were bad with money, which trickled down to them and will stop with you. This might not work; they might just be too resistant to change, and that is when you find the quickest way to exit because it is toxic. They are recklessly draining your money without any regard for your life, and you have to enter survival mode. That is no place for anyone to be, but circumstances like this do exist. The relationship between you and your parents might be strained but protecting your own money must be your priority. Hopefully, after some time, everyone can forgive and let live. Be sure to pay close attention to how they respond to you, though. That response will be very telling.

Getting someone into a good place financially is one thing, but keeping him or her there, so they don't continue to ask you for money can be significantly more difficult. You can't hold their hand forever, and they need to know that. This is temporary, and you get to say, "I have taught you how to fish, so there are no more excuses." Before you let them go, it might be a good idea for you to look at how much debt they might be in then find out if they have life insurance and what their retirement plans are. If you can set them up to where they will be independent, you will both be in a better spot down the line.

Chapter 19: Salary

I received a job offer and intended to accept it because it was my only offer. Like most people, I tried to calculate what my weekly pay would be minus taxes and deductions. The next day, I received another job offer of around $5,000 more on the base than the first job offer, so naturally, I had to choose. I liked the job paying less money better than the other, but $5,000 is nothing to turn my nose up at. Still, then I noticed something playing with the salary calculator. After taxes and medical deductions, the take-home pay difference between the two was marginal. Not enough of a real difference for me to choose one over the other for purely monetary reasons. I say that to show you not to look at just the salary but to make take-home pay the priority, especially if you're in my situation and have multiple offers. Figure out the exact pay difference and use that to negotiate a higher offer. Just because the take-home pay may be minimal between one job and the other, it doesn't mean that your actual salary isn't important. There can be substantial differences in many cases. A higher salary means a higher starting point for negotiations if you pursue another job.

Another important thing to consider is the benefits your job provides. Benefits are a good way to identify how much the company cares about its employees. Salaries are easy to throw at people because that is the main deciding factor, and employers know it. But benefits are a little less of a concern, especially for millennials. Understanding if the company has their own health insurance or not and the deductible cost. Understanding if they will cover your spouse and for how much and your children are also important. Many companies put the choice in your hands regarding which pre-tax benefits you want to contribute towards, and some help with that. These include a flexible spending account, a health savings account, and life insurance as well. All of those are pre-tax benefits that lower your taxable income. These benefits, as well as others, are usually called cafeteria plan benefits.

Retirement options such as 401(k) or pensions and understanding which one an employer offers plus the pros and cons of each should influence a job decision. Matching is also something to look out for. Knowing how much their company match is and offering a Roth 401(k) plan will save you money down the road. Their vesting period can also be important, depending on its length. A shorter vesting period to get to 100% is most preferable just because if you leave sooner than later, you don't have to worry about not receiving your match. Paid time off is different for everyone depending on his or her point in life. I know people who never use any of theirs and people who use every bit of it plus purchase PTO days, but only you will know how much that means to you. What is becoming more popular is discretionary time off where you don't have a defined amount of PTO days. Instead, you take them when you need them. This is good for employees and companies because I know people who take PTO days only not to lose them, which can be inconvenient. Not only is PTO important, but maternity/paternity leave plus other medical leave as well. U.S. Companies are starting to adopt the ideologies of other developed countries in terms of paid leave. This might not be an immediate benefit, but it can be down the line. If you are considering furthering your education, understanding their tuition assistance program, such as how much they will pay and how long you must commit to them after you're finished, is important as well. One of my favorite perks is working remotely. The nature of what I do can be done all from a laptop, so there is no real reason to come into the office every day. With the advent of Skype business, Zoom, and other communications methods, it makes your job remotely much easier. This makes work a lot easier, more flexible and saves you commute time. While this is more common, it is still important to know how a company looks at remote work. It may only be role or team specific. Some companies will let certain employees work from home once a week, others on an as-needed basis, even as low as once a month or not at all. I worked a job where one of my coworkers permanently worked from home, so it is possible. Another employee worked in another country just because he always wanted to live there. As you can see, this can be beneficial but again, understand how a company looks at it. Because of technology, there's no real reason we need to be in the office as much as we are, and I think jobs will be more remote as time goes on. There are drawbacks if a company is too progressive regarding remote work. You miss that human interaction that creates cohesion and synergy with your team, especially with your boss, which is important for promotions and recognition.

When I got my offer, one thing I didn't do is negotiate my salary. The first reason was that I asked for something else and didn't feel comfortable asking for a salary increase at that time. The other reason was that it was already more than they initially said the position was worth. It was already within the salary range I was seeking anyway. I considered it a win. Despite this, I still should've asked for more money. Even if I didn't get it, at least I'd have tried. Don't be me. Always negotiate. In my situation, I had a certain career experience that was rare and relevant to my current job. I could've used that to justify requesting a higher salary. Since I didn't ask, I don't know if the salary was even negotiable in the first place. They could've said this salary is non-negotiable, and that would've ended all talks right there, but it can't hurt you to ask. And even if the salary wasn't negotiable, maybe the benefits were. I could've gotten another week of vacation or a multitude of other things. If the salary wasn't negotiable, then I should've asked the criteria for raises and promotions. How an annual raise is determined also wasn't conveyed either, but that is important because some companies do not give annual raises. But if they do, ask what the range you can expect. Negotiation doesn't stop at the job offer. There may be times where you feel you deserve a raise for either the extra value you've added or the extra work you've taken on. Picking the right time to ask is imperative. Performance reviews and before after completing big projects is a perfect time as well. When asking, you can't just have a random number; you have to identify how you arrived at whatever amount you want. Whether it's relative to an industry average or based on the work, you've been doing, especially if your team is newly understaffed. The number you ask for is important because you might have to compromise. This isn't necessarily a bad thing because sometimes the raise isn't about the money. Asking for a raise shows confidence and poise to your manager and sets the tone that you're serious about compensation. That alone is worth it, but the money is obviously the key to all of this. I don't want to stay at my current company, so there is no reason for me to leverage an offer with them for more money. If I did, having an offer from another company does help when asking for a raise, even if you don't intend to take the other job. This tells you and your current employer that you know how much you're worth on the open market. That is power. The wording is up to you, but you want to have an offer and express you'd like to stay with your current company but would like more money to stay. I think it's always good to interview, even if you are pleased with your current job, to know what's out there and keep you sharp. Remember, your salary is important, but benefits are also important, so don't get hung up too much on one or the other.

Chapter 20: 401(k)

Your 401(k) is one of if not the most important vehicles to save and invest for retirement. It takes a lot of responsibility from the individual if you don't touch it. The process is largely seamless. That might be a problem because you don't know how much is there and how much you contribute to each check, and maybe what you're invested in. It's best to start contributing 15% of your salary to your 401(k), then have an annual increase of 1% if you deem it necessary but at minimum 15%. These are important things you should be checking at least yearly. Most companies also have a projected income calculator that can help you see what your retirement could look like, which is just an estimation that doesn't really account for promotions or changing jobs/careers. However, it's still good to see, especially when you check it yearly.

I'm sure we're all familiar with a company match, usually around 3-6%, just free money for working there. Still, some might not know that companies might have a vesting period. A vesting period means that you must work a certain amount of time before you're eligible to receive the company match or receive the full company match. By full company match, I mean that companies might have a vesting schedule where every year, usually on your work anniversary or hire date, you're eligible for more of the match. For example, you will be eligible for 20% at year one, so you will receive $0.20 from the company for every dollar you contribute. In year two, it might be 40% and so on. Other vesting periods might be designed where you are eligible for none of the match for years one and two. At year three, you're eligible for 100% of the company match. Companies sometimes vary on how their vesting schedule is set up. It's important to know which one yours is just if you decide to quit a week before your vesting period ends. I was offered a new job. They wanted me to start two weeks before I would've been eligible for the full company match as I was not eligible for that in the first two years. To clarify, your vesting period isn't like an annual raise; it's more like if you decide to leave, this is how much your company will honor. You're earning the full match until you leave, then it is decided how much you will take with you. If you decide to leave and then return, be sure to know if your previous years of service will count toward your vesting period or not as well.

Most don't know what their 401(k) contribution is invested in. This can be detrimental to your returns if it's not reviewed at least yearly. Your age is a large factor in how your portfolio should be balanced, as your risk tolerance should change as time goes on. A 22-year-old fresh out of college should be heavily leveraged in aggressive investments. A 50-year-old should be heavily leveraged in more conservative investments. Over the 30-35 years before you retire or start taking out distributions, the stock market is going to have a few major swings like it did when COVID-19 happened or when the stock market crashed in 2008. Someone in the earlier stages of their career can weather these highs and lows because it's over such a long period of time, and they will have time to recover when the market dips. That is why it makes sense to be more aggressive in your greener years. A 55-year-old can't weather those dips as easily as they have less time before they retire. They are more conservative, so market volatility doesn't affect their 401(k).

Picking what you want to invest in isn't as hard as you think. Most people are not invested in the stock market outside of their 401(k), so it's completely foreign. Fortunately, the company that your job uses to manage your 401(k) makes this simple, hopefully. You will have to do some research on your own, and it's not something you do quickly, but from the funds you are allowed to pick from, they will show you a 1-year, 5-year, and 10-year rate of return for that fund. Use this information to make your decision. You won't pick individual stocks typically, which is generally good because too much choice is a bad thing. You will generally have the option of picking from a basket of funds like target-date funds. For the most part, it's not a hard task. It just takes a little time and education. Don't be afraid to educate yourself about your money. At the very least, get on the phone and talk to someone at the company that manages your company's 401(k). I'm sure they'd be happy to help. Finally, don't forget to look at it every year to see if you need to make any changes.

Most are familiar with the traditional 401(k), but a relatively new type of 401(k) is called a Roth 401(k). With a traditional 401(k), the taxes you pay are deferred, and you pay taxes on the money when you retire. With a Roth 401(k), you pay tax on the money upfront, so when you take it out at retirement, you pay no taxes because you paid on it already. To break it down, assume you're 25, and you make $1,800 a month, which is $75 a check, and with some quick math, at age 65, you'll have contributed $72,000 before tax and income tax at your current age is 10%. With a traditional 401(k), you didn't pay tax on that $72,000, and it grew, let's say grew at 5% with compound interest at retirement for a total of $223,285. At that point, you will be taxed on the money you take out at whatever your tax rate in which we will just keep it at 10%, that means the growth is also taxed, so of that $151,285 of gains you made is taxed at ten or more percent. Still, we'll say 10% as well, so you lost $22,328 to taxes off the gain because you decided to pay taxes later. Take that same $75 you invested net of taxes because you paid the taxes upfront. The money you would receive at retirement is $223,285. Now I used the 10% tax rate for the 30 years, but that was just an assumption. The tax rate at the beginning of your career and the end of your career will more than likely not stay the same, and even if it does, your tax bracket might not be the same either. You need to ask yourself if you think the income tax or your tax bracket will change when you choose between a Roth or a Traditional. In this example, I didn't account for a company match because you must pay tax on that when you retire regardless of the plan you choose.

Speaking of leaving your company for a new one, what happens to your 401(k)? Well, you have a few options. Each option depends on your individual situation. If you leave your company for a new company, you can either keep your 401(k) at your old company if you have more than $5,000 or move it to your new company after finding out when you are eligible to participate in their 401(k). You can also roll it over into an IRA. You can also take cash payment, but you'd be subject to a penalty and will be taxed as well, so this is usually frowned upon.

When you're young and might have a good amount of student loan or credit card debt, it might be a good idea to forego your 401(k) contributions to pay down debt. However, that takes a lot of discipline, so if you don't think you'll use that money to pay off debt, don't do it and just invest in your 401(k). The reason this is practical is that you'll have plenty of time to invest in a 401(k) and the stock market and whatever else. A five-year hiatus in contributions where that money is going to debt is a viable solution. If you're under 25, you have about 40 years to work before retirement, so five or so years to pay off debt is fine.

Epilogue: Sacrifice

For two years straight, I worked between 70-75 hours a week. I'd wake up at 8 am and work my first job from 9 am to 5 pm. I'd leave my first job at 5 pm, drive Uber for five hours, and then get home at 10-11 pm, eat and go to sleep and do it again. This was my life Monday through

Thursday and even longer on Friday because I'd usually get off early and drive Uber for longer. Same for the weekend, I'd work 5-8 hours of Uber, sometimes twice in a day. Through this, I was able to pay my rent, utilities, groceries, and car payments for the month with Uber alone. On top of this, I still had a paycheck from my regular job. I amassed a great deal of money (which I wish I were a little smarter with). And built up a good amount in savings and investments to the point where money was not an object. I saved and invested a lot of money, but I also enjoyed a lot of money. I love to travel, so that's mostly what it helped fund. I was on a plane once a month, and the best part about it is, I never had to check my bank account afterward out of fear. I made a sacrifice. I said no to many happy hours because that was prime moneymaking time. One New Year's Eve, as the clock struck 12 am, I was telling a guy from New York with a computer science degree that I was driving to the MGM Grand, Happy New Year. I sacrificed a lot of time and missed out on quite a few events. Still, two years later, I had a nice savings account and investing account all because of sacrifice. And my favorite thing about my sacrifice was, I didn't have to. I was fine with just my first job, but the second job provided me the extra cushion I always wanted for myself. So, what are you willing to sacrifice for your future?

Time is your biggest asset if you utilize it and your worst enemy if you waste it. Tomorrow is coming whether you're ready for it or not. Don't assume your health will always be the same, either. We take our health for granted, and it is not guaranteed. Tomorrow won't care. I know some of you are in bad financial shape because that's what the data says and because some of these people are my friends and family. I've seen how my friends operate financially from high school to college to now, and some don't seem ever to learn. I consistently see them deciding to buy a new car with bad credit and a 16% interest rate plus high insurance premiums. Why do you think you deserve this car? What is this doing for you? Some never say no to a night out and have to be a part of every vacation and have credit card debt with no nest egg while living paycheck to paycheck.

I believe that your twenties are supposed to be the worst years of your adult life. You're possibly in school or just graduating. You are an adult, but you also still depend on your parents financially. You're trying to figure out a career path that is forever changing. You've probably had a few jobs in a short amount of time. You're trying to climb the ladder at your job and compete in the great American rat race. Not to mention student loan debt. It's just a weird time because it's so much ambiguity. My twenties are full of regrets financially and personally, and if I knew then what I knew now, I'd be so much better off. With a lot more clarity and a lot more money, but it wouldn't be life if that was possible. At the end of my twenties, the light is knowing that my thirties will be much better and forties even better than my thirties. How about you? Will the next decade of your life be better, worse, or the same as your previous decade? If the answer is worse or the same, then you probably have some work to do. I think you can't figure out if it will be the same or worse until you are towards the end of that period. Once you know that the next decade is looking bleak, that is when you should sacrifice the remaining years of the current decade and lock-in. Do whatever you have to do to make that next period in your life better. If that means no vacations and a lot of overtime, then so be it. If it means no dating, clubs, and restaurants, then that is what it takes. With sacrifice, in the future, you will be much happier, I promise. Temporary stress for permanent success should be your mantra.

Maybe we are too tied to one place because maybe it's our hometown and all our family and friends are there, or we moved there for career or school reasons. Still, that city and/or state financially doesn't make sense. I know in a few cities and states, the cost of living is ridiculous, but we still stay. Los Angeles is in the news once a week for their rising rent and homeowner costs paired with the homelessness rate, not to mention the earthquakes, wildfires, and droughts. I can't figure out why people stay there. There are pockets of great cities for whatever stage of life you're in that are much cheaper. Maybe consider moving to a less expensive city or state, even if it's just temporarily.

We all have short-term and long-term goals that ignore our financial situations. Marriage and children are our goals, but you can't afford a wedding without going into debt and wouldn't dare go to the courthouse. We can't afford a ring, but we wouldn't dare to wear our wedding bands. They would rather have a wedding that they go into debt to have than have a down payment for their house. You can have all the things you want, desire, and then some, but something has to give. These temporary things have long-lasting consequences.

As you get older, you don't want to work harder out of necessity. Still, the track some of you are on, you're going to be playing catch up when more is at stake. Two jobs at forty years old with kids is not a life anyone wants. Would it hurt that much to sacrifice the next two years with very little to no fun or relaxation? Two years of working overtime or part-time, no eating out, no leisure activities, no traveling, no alcohol, and no dating if you're not married with all the money after bills going to either debt or a nest egg. I know that might be hard to imagine, but just think about the past two years and think about how much money you spent on pleasure and food, then think about how well just half of that would look like in your bank account. I promise you this is not a decision you will regret in two years.

In 2008, Hurricane Ike ravaged the Gulf of Mexico on the Bolivar Peninsula. It destroyed everything on the coast except one home known as the 'Last House Standing.' This house was the only house standing because the couple that occupied the house experienced a hurricane before. In 2005, hurricane Maria hit them in the same place as in 2008, but they were prepared this time. They rebuilt their house in the same place but this time with the proper materials to withstand a hurricane. This applies to you. You might have your own hurricane Ike. It can be something like the 2008 financial crisis, and you lose your job, or it could be you get sick and get overwhelmed by medical bills. The COVID-19 pandemic might have caused you to get laid off. If your current financial situation is bad, it will worsen when you have to weather a storm. Build yourself up with savings, emergency funds, investments, insurance, and everything else I've discussed in this book. When the hurricane hit the house the second time, they still had minor repairs to make, even with them using the right materials. However, the foundation of the house was still standing and strong. They were prepared. Your storm will come. When it does, will you be a pile of wood, bricks and tiles on the ground or the last house standing?

How Much Value Are You Getting from Your Car?

Yearly Car Payment _____

Yearly Insurance Cost_____

Yearly Registration_____

Yearly City Sticker_____

Yearly Oil Change Cost_____

Yearly Maintence Cost_____

Yearly Traffic Violation Ticket_____

Yearly Depreciation_____

Accident Deducible (if applicable)_____

Yearly Cost Total_____x4%_____ <-Yearly Value

*4% is the average usage received from a car

I would like to extend a special thank you to the following for consultation during writing this book

Kevin Annang

Marcus Belin

Darrin Davis

Airen Foney

Crystal Foney

Alicia Foster

Ebony Holder

Chardeney Mason

Justin McClinton

Takeya McCollum

Adarious Payton

Todd Sparkman

Jeremiah Williams

Charonn Woods

Crystal Woods

Works Cited

"8 Criteria for Evaluating a Job Offer : Look Before You Leap." *Skills Training From MindTools.com*, www.mindtools.com/pages/article/evaluating-job-offer.htm.

Appleby, Denise. "Job Hunting: Higher Pay vs Better Benefits." *Www.investopedia.com*, 25 May 2020, www.investopedia.com/articles/retirement/09/job-retirement-benefits.asp.

Cohen, Aubrey. "What to Do When Your Term Life Insurance Expires." *NerdWallet*, 15 Dec. 2020, www.nerdwallet.com/blog/insurance/term-life-insurance-expires-extend-convert/.

Crouch, Michelle. "Can a Prenup or Postnup Save You from a Spouse's Debt?" *Foxbusiness.com*, 18 Apr. 2017, www.foxbusiness.com/features/can-a-prenup-or-postnup-save- you-from-a-spouses-debt.amp.

Danise, Amy. "The Best Life Insurance Companies 2021." *Forbes*, Forbes Magazine, 6 Jan. 2021, www.forbes.com/sites/barbaramarquand/2016/01/27/the-hows-and-whys-of-life-insurance-for-children/#53fb9c144511.

Heinig, Melissa. "Prenuptial Agreements: What Does the Law Allow?" *Www.nolo.com*, Nolo, 24 Jan. 2020, www.nolo.com/legal-encyclopedia/prenuptial-agreements-what-law-allows-30283.html.

"How to Make an Offer on a House in 7 Steps: Zillow." *Home Buyers Guide*, 26 Oct. 2020, www.zillow.com/home-buying-guide/making-an-offer-on-a-house/.

Jeanie, Skowronski, and Patrick Hanzel. "Is Life Insurance for Children Worth It?" *Policygenius*, 24 July 2020, www.policygenius.com/life-insurance/life-insurance-for-children/.

Krome, Charles. "Car Depreciation: How Much Value Will a New Car Lose?" *CARFAX*, 5 Feb. 2019, www.carfax.com/blog/car-depreciation.

Lake, Rebecca. "5 Mistakes to Avoid When Paying Off Your Mortgage Early." *SmartAsset*, SmartAsset, 24 Mar. 2020, smartasset.com/mortgage/mistakes-to-avoid-when-paying-off-your-mortgage-early##targetText=Basics%20of%20Paying%20Your%20Mortgage%20Early&targetText=There%20are%20a%20few%20different,can%20go%20about%20paying%20early.&targetText=You%20can%20also%20increase%20your,loan%20to%20a%20shorter%20term.

Lake, Rebecca. "Buying a Home: Do You Need Title Insurance?" *SmartAsset*, SmartAsset, 9 July 2019, smartasset.com/mortgage/buying-a-home-do-you-need-title-insurance.

LaPonsie, Maryalene. "How to Talk - Not Fight - About Money With Your Spouse." *NerdWallet*, 15 Nov. 2017, www.nerdwallet.com/article/finance/how-to-talk-about-money-with-your-spouse.

Leonhardt, Megan. "Americans Spend over $1,000 a Year on Lotto Tickets." *CNBC*, CNBC, 12 Dec. 2019, www.cnbc.com/2019/12/12/americans-spend-over-1000-dollars-a-year-on-lotto-tickets.html#:~:text=Consumers%20each%20spend%20an%20average,Powerball%20and%20Mega%20Millions%20competitions.

Luthi, Ben. "Bank or Dealership: What's the Best Way to Finance a Car?" *Experian*, Experian, 11 Oct. 2019, www.experian.com/blogs/ask-experian/is-it-better-to-finance-a-car-through-a-bank-or-dealership/.

The National Study of Millionaires: Findings from the Research Study behind Everyday Millionaires, by Chris Hogan, Ramsey Press, 2020.

Parker, Tim. "The Cost of Raising a Child in the United States." *Investopedia*, Investopedia, 28 Aug. 2020, www.investopedia.com/articles/personal-finance/090415/cost-raising-child-america.asp.

Wamala, Yowana. "Fixed vs. Variable Interest Rates: What's the Difference?" *ValuePenguin*, ValuePenguin, 10 Dec. 2019, www.valuepenguin.com/loans/fixed-vs-variable-interest-rates##targetText=A%20fixed%20rate%20loan%20has,won't%20change%20in%20cost.

"What Is Owner's Title Insurance?" *Consumer Financial Protection Bureau*, www.consumerfinance.gov/ask-cfpb/what-is-owners-title-insurance-en-164/##targetText=Owner's%20title%20insurance%20provides%20protection,before%20the%20homeowner%20purchased%20it.&targetText=Most%20le

nders%20require%20you%20to,protects%20the%20amount%20they%20lend.

Disclaimer: The views and opinions expressed in the book are solely views and opinions and should not be taken as professional or legal advice.

www.ingramcontent.com/pod-product-compliance
Lightning Source LLC
Chambersburg PA
CBHW071128240526
45465CB00024B/1546